Teaching Troubled and Troublesome Adolescents

Teaching Troubled and Troublesome Adolescents

Jane Lovey

David Fulton Publishers Ltd
London
Published in association with the Roehampton Institute

David Fulton Publishers Ltd
2 Barbon Close, London WC1N 3JX

First published in Great Britain by
David Fulton Publishers 1992

British Library Cataloguing in Publication Data

A catalogue record for this book is available from the British Library

ISBN 1-85346-194-6

Typeset by Chapterhouse, Formby, L37 3PX
Printed in Great Britain by BPCC Wheaton Ltd. Exeter

Contents

DEDICATION

This book is dedicated to my mother, Anne Porter, whose strong example taught me that challenges were there to be faced and problems were there to be solved.

Acknowledgements

I would like to express my thanks to Jim Docking for his encouragement and his patience in editing the text of this book. I am also grateful to Bob Gale in Leicester and Pat Reid in Brighton who shared with me their experiences of planning programmes for adolescents in cooperation with their own schools. My thanks also to Alan Kimbell in Sutton who has supported me constantly in the work described in this book.

I also acknowledge the help given to me by my sons, Jose, Peter and Andrew, and their cousin Emma, who, in their comparatively untroubled passage through adolescence, have shared their hopes and thoughts with me.

Introduction

For the last 12 years I have been privileged to teach some of the most troublesome and troubled adolescents from schools in my borough. I say that I have been privileged because I have not had to cope with them in classes of 20, 30 or more, I have not had outside pressure on me to ensure they pass examinations, and I have not had to insist on their obedience to a set of rules. This is because I have taught these pupils in a small off-site unit where there are rarely more than 15 pupils at any one time, and they are taught, by three of us, in groups of not more than seven.

I realise that we are dealing with the tip of the iceberg and for every one we teach in the unit there are probably four or more others who would benefit from what we have to offer. There are many pupils, sitting reasonably quietly in their classrooms, who would greatly benefit from having much more individual teaching and support of the kind that only those actually disrupting the class enough to be removed will receive. Often it is only one final act of defiance or insubordination, and this not necessarily in the classroom, that will entitle the excluded or expelled pupil to the special kind of education provided in a unit.

Since the implementation of the Warnock report (DES, 1978), with its emphasis on the desirability of all children, if at all possible, remaining integrated within mainstream schools, authorities have been looking closely at alternatives to isolating disrupting pupils in special off-site units. The presence of special needs coordinators has provided an opportunity for teachers to discuss with a named professional within the school, strategies for dealing with pupils who are beginning to present management problems.

Authorities are questioning the place of these off-site units in the educational provision. There are a number of anomalies in the running of most of these units because of the ad hoc way in which most were set up in response to a crisis situation. Some were under the aegis of Social Services and others were an adjunct to the Home Tuition Service, some

1

were on the site of the feeder secondary schools, others off-site and taking pupils from several schools. In the late 1970s and early 1980s many started out as Intermediate Treatment Units.

Now the pendulum has swung. Units that mushroomed a dozen years ago are being closed for financial (LMS) and philosophical (Warnock) reasons. My unit has already closed and is being replaced by a Secondary Behavioural Support Service which will concentrate resources on Outreach work which will provide earlier, in-school intervention. The focus of work with year-11 pupils who are out of school is based on accessing resources in the community, such as work experience, voluntary work and college courses. It is hoped that it will be possible to keep more of these special pupils in their high schools by offering them and their teachers on-site support. Some of the teachers being recruited for Outreach are teachers with experience in units. It is my earnest hope that the unique experience we have been able to gain in units will not be wasted once these units are closed. The Elton Report (DES, 1989) acknowledges that pupils in units are dependent on the special skills of the teachers in them, if they are to work successfully and increase their future prospects (6:47) and, expresses regret that 'Because these units are isolated from the system as a whole, those skills are seldom passed on to other teachers'.

Since they risk losing so much from their removal, I think it is useful to look closely at why these pupils have problems in mainstream schools. How much of the problem is the emotional luggage they bring in to school with them each day, and how much is to do with classroom dynamics or teaching methods?

In writing this I am very conscious that many of the strategies we have used in the unit would not be possible in a busy mainstream school with a much less favourable staff-pupil ratio. Also some strategies which worked for our pupils would not be appropriate for pupils who are able to function in a more mature, self-assured manner. However, I think that it is useful to look at how some of the ostensibly least teachable of our adolescents can be reached by less conventional methods. I hope that this will help other teachers who encounter these disturbed and disturbing youngsters to understand a little more of what is going on inside the child. In particular, I feel it is worth remembering that teachers are often on the receiving end of anger and frustration that has been brought in from home. Often the teacher is the most stable and the safest person in the child's life. It is important that we treat these pupils with the dignity we afford to their well-behaved peers while recognising their undoubted infantile needs.

CHAPTER 1

Adolescent – Child or Adult?

In this age of mass communication, when any incident of violence or student protest is relayed to the nation in inescapable half-hourly news bulletins, the populace could be excused for fearing, at times, that discipline among the nation's young has totally broken down. That the majority of pupils in the majority of schools behave most of the time with due regard to the rules of the establishment is hardly likely to make even the back page of any newspaper: however that is the fact. Nevertheless, it cannot be denied that there are a few children in nearly every school who offer a daily challenge to their teachers and who arouse the concern of those responsible for their education, and the education of the children who share the same classrooms.

Troublesome adolescents – an age old problem

Perhaps it is of comfort to some of us to realise that troublesome behaviour in adolescence is not a new problem. The disruptive behaviour of pupils and students throughout the ages is well documented (Lawson and Silver, 1973). On 12 September 1911, London schoolboys went on strike for the abolition of the cane and an extra half day's holiday. It was also around this time, in the Lambeth area of London, that Patrick Houligan, with his band of wild friends (all adolescents) gave his name to the behaviour which we know today. With today's efficient mass communication system knowledge of this would have been more widespread, and presumably more widely imitated in the provinces.

Adolescence – a time of risks and daring

Perhaps it would be true to say that disruption is not so much a sign of the times as a manifestation of adolescence. It is necessary to look at

3

adolescence as a stage through which all humans pass in order to make sense of adolescent behaviour. It is at this age that many of the Crusaders went out to fight passionately for their faith in the twelfth and thirteenth centuries. This activity provided a valid outlet for adolescent energies and satisfied the desire to prove courage and independence – an ability to function without parental support. One hears of little disruptive behaviour during the two world wars when young men had a legitimate outlet for their energies which gave them acceptable public status.

My pupils are enthralled by the writings of Colin Perry, a local man, in his *Boy in the Blitz*. He describes in flowery and heroic language his feelings when cycling around our local south London area and observing bombs dropping and planes overhead. He speculates on his proximity to death and scorns those neighbours who follow government instructions and miss the thrills of risk in order to sit out a raid in a shelter. They are amused by the affected language and patriotic sentiments, but also impressed by the foolhardiness of this young man. Perhaps it is a matter for regret that, in a society that is increasingly concerned with health and safety legislation, there are few legitimate opportunities to take risks and prove one's courage.

In more natural societies, particularly in Africa, even in these days of increased education and technology, the male initiation and circumcision ceremonies are still important, although wild-life protection legislation has emasculated some aspects of the ritual. Proving the ability to endure pain without flinching remains an essential process in the formal passage from child to man.

In our own society the factory or work place initiation 'ceremony' can be a humiliating rather than daring experience, although it may be potentially dangerous and damaging to body and spirit. Because pupils are now kept at school beyond the physical changes from child to adult, the transition from dependant to wage earner does not coincide with coping with new adult feelings.

Adolescence – a normal stage of development

Here it is useful to look at adolescence as a stage of human development. Just as it is believed that what happens during infancy has great importance for the development of the personality and has certain irreversible influences, so do the experiences of adolescence have a vital bearing on later life.

The psychoanalytic theory of adolescence sees it as a period when the personality is extremely vulnerable, resulting from the upsurge of instincts at puberty. It is recognised that there is a risk of maladaptive behaviour because of the inadequacy of psychological defences to cope with inner conflicts and tensions. This can cause extreme fluctuations of mood, inconsistency in relationships, depression and non-conformity. It is also a time of emotional, if not physical, separation from parents, if mature emotional and sexual relationships are to be formed outside the home. From this theory comes the psychiatric model of identity crisis and such severe adolescent turmoil that it manifests itself as an illness to be treated in a hospital or clinic. Some adolescents in special units have reached this stage and are being educated in units connected with psychiatric hospitals or remand homes. Whether an adolescent with a psychiatric label is consigned to an adolescent unit or a remand home is often not merely a question of whether or not offences have been committed, but how those offences have been dealt with. This can be dependent on such factors as socio-economic category, area of residence, reports of professionals, family reputation and the ability to be represented by a sympathetic and competent solicitor.

Sociological theories look at external influences on the developing adolescent rather than internal forces, particularly socialization and role. Socialization is seen as being the process by which individuals in society absorb the values, standards and beliefs current in that society. Much of this will be to do with recognising one's role in the family, and knowing the expectations of that role. According to this perspective adolescence is the move from the ascribed roles of childhood to the choice of roles, and the interpretation of those roles, which are available to the maturing boy or girl.

Adolescents and thinking

Piaget (1959) pointed out that, in adolescence, there is a qualitative change in the nature of mental ability rather than a simple increase in cognitive skill, and that this is the state of development where formal operational thought becomes possible. With this comes the ability to reason things out and form an opinion. It is a time when theories can be discussed and weighed up and there is some understanding of possibility and probability. Needless to say not all adolescents reach this cognitive stage at the same age, and many never reach it. In some cases this may be because of a lack of endowed intelligence, although it is believed that this is only a very small factor governing cognitive development. The more important factors are probably type of school, attitude of the teachers, self-image, achievement, motivation, position in the peer group, parental attitudes and home environment.

The importance of careful cognitive intervention at this stage is paramount. It is a major responsibility for those who teach adolescents to ensure that they are helped to develop their ability to think and reason. It may be the last time in life that this kind of intervention is available to the young person. When preparing work for my group of pupils my aim is to present material which will make them want to think for themselves.

One important aspect of adolescent reasoning is the individual's egocentrism which makes it very difficult for him or her to differentiate between what others are thinking about and his or her own preoccupations. As every parent will know, adolescents are very preoccupied with their appearance, spending hours in front of a mirror and always anticipating criticism from others. There is enormous fear of not fitting in with the peer group. It is egocentrism that also influences the adolescent's 'story of his or her self', which is how he or she thinks his or her imaginary audiences sees them. Needless to say, this sensitivity to the real or imagined criticism from the peer group affects much of an adolescent's behaviour and aspirations in school. The conflicts caused by examinations at this stage are discussed in Chapter 6.

The needs of adolescents in today's society

Coleman (1980, p. 187) summarises the needs of adolescents in society today:

> Adolescents do need adults to take some responsibility and have some clear and reasonable rules, without being too authoritarian.
>
> Young people have a need to participate in the adult world as fully as possible, especially in the world of work. The less involvement there is then the more adolescent will be vulnerable to peer pressure.
>
> Adolescents need to be seen as individuals, not just part of 'youth' and adults will only have rewarding relationships with adolescents if they treat them as individual people rather than part of a 'movement'.
>
> Adolescents will only reach their full potential in cognitive development if helped and encouraged to do so by the adults around them. They do need help with intellectual development as much as social development.
>
> Teenagers need more help with their developing sexuality with both

social and sex education. Young people need the opportunity to take part in peer group activities as it is from their peers that they learn new social skills. But they need to have a firm parental base as a reinforcing agency of socialization.

Rather than concentrating on the problems of adolescence Coleman focuses on the need for *support* of young people who are passing from the dependency of childhood to the accountability of adult life. Just as it is important to treat adolescents who sometimes, because of the importance of fitting in with their peer group, seem to be part of an amorphous movement, as individuals, it is also important to respect adolescent non-conformity, even though it can lead to unpredictable, or even impossible behaviour.

Adolescence and adult fears

Teachers in adolescent units are often greeted with gasps of amazement and admiration when they reveal how they earn their living. Parents of adolescents immediately start relating tales of the perceived unreasonable behaviour of their own adolescent off-spring yet few adults seem to remember their own adolescence with any degree of accuracy.

The response of older people makes it evident how threatening even small groups of adolescents can seem. Part of this is caused by the noise of the loud, unmodulated, newly adult voices of the boys, the shrieks of the girls and the almost inevitable 'music machine' that will be present. Adolescents often have an uncontrolled gait, and are not always enough in control of their rapidly lengthening limbs to avoid some involuntary conflict with passers-by. Because at my unit we shared a common entrance gate with the ambulant members of a Senior Citizens Day Centre, I tried to help my pupils to understand how they appear to the frail and the elderly, especially those who have read the popular press.

Because our playground is used as a five-a-side football pitch in the evening, it is surrounded by a 10-foot fence. So that equipment may be left out overnight the doors to the 'cage' have heavy padlocks on them; it is also equipped with floodlighting. The purpose of the fencing and floodlighting was obviously misunderstood by neighbours who, having lost their petition against our occupation of the premises, watched us move in with concerned interest. At lunch-time on the first day I received an amused call from the education offices. One of our neighbours had rung to say that a gate had been left unlocked and he had seen 'two of the delinquents escape!' Fortunately they had been reassured by the office, but there has always been a certain nervousness.

On another occasion, during a long, hot summer, our boys were delighted to espy a neighbour sunbathing in the nude. They spotted her when they went to retrieve a tennis ball that had strayed over the playground fence and into our car park. It appears that when they bent to retrieve the ball near the hedge where it had come to a halt, they were rewarded with an unexpected eyeful. Obviously this was too good to waste and before I knew what was happening all the boys were sharing the welcome bonus. Since they were still on the unit's territory and on the other side of the lady's fence, there was no question of trespass (except by the eyes). Nevertheless the neighbour reported our boys to the office as perverts who were totally out of control. There was no concession to the fact that it might not be wise to sunbathe in the raw, in a tiny suburban garden, less then ten metres from a school for adolescents, let alone those presenting behaviour problems.

Another time I received enquiries about why a police car had been on our site. I was mystified since we had had a quiet afternoon with no visits from the police. It later transpired that two elderly gentlemen at the Day Centre had been involved in a disagreement about a game of cards and had set about each other with their walking sticks prompting the manager to call the police. When I related the story to our youngsters they were very amused and viewed our elderly neighbours with increased respect!

In many ways the head of a unit takes on many of the roles of a caring parent during the day. On the rare occasions that confrontations between pupils, or between pupil and teacher occur, they are conducted in front of a suspicious and prejudiced audience from the surrounding semis and other local authority centres. The car park is used by all departments and we share the site with not only a Day Centre for the elderly, but also one for the mentally handicapped, plus a day nursery, and units for Adult Literacy, home tuition and occupational therapy. Raised voices in our playground have the same effect as the shout of 'there's a fight' during a school playtime. Spectators suddenly appear.

I have to demonstrate that I am in control. I do this best by trying to elicit information about the dispute from other pupils. If this is done quietly enough everyone else has to be quiet so that they know what is going on. By using this strategy the noise level is usually reduced and I am able to say to one or the other of the individuals involved, or occasionally both, that I can understand the anger. If it seems agreed that an injustice has been done I will offer to sort it out myself. If tempers are very frayed I might have to send a pupil home until the next day, but, to be fair, I must make sure I send home the one who has started it, not necessarily the one who is making most noise. It is better if, as often happens, all three of our staff work together, so that two talk to each of the protagonists individually and the third teacher occupies and listens to those not involved. The important thing is that something is seen to be done, the reason for the dispute is seen to be addressed, and the business is finished during that session. If a fight is simply stopped and the pupils corralled whilst still angry, no work is achieved and the trouble starts again outside the unit at the end of the day, thereby fulfilling the neighbours' expectations of 'that kind of teenager'.

Perhaps I am lucky. I have never been hit or caught in the cross-fire in 12 and a half years in this situation. I have only twice been aware of a pupil being in possession of an offensive weapon. In both cases these were girls who were swiftly disarmed, and their parents were called in. I think it is important that pupils realise that we are very vigilant and aware of the possibility of weapons; but more important is the knowledge that there are strong adults in control, who apply a known set of principles and procedures to every situation.

Educational provision for adolescent problems

The appropriateness of removing disaffected adolescents from mainstream schooling has always been controversial, but since the 1981 Education Act there has been even more unease about this policy. This is because the emphasis now is on the integration of children into mainstream schooling where traditionally their needs were met by special school provision. However, there is the proviso in this Act that special educational needs should only be met in mainstream schools if this ensures efficient use of resources *and is not detrimental to the needs of other children in the school.*

In his discussion about this problem Laslett (1977) advocates Outreach work. There are a number of such projects already in place. I describe these initiatives in Chapter 7. Nevertheless there is a group of pupils, usually in the fourth or fifth forms, who have become so disaffected from school that they are unlikely to be present in school, or the level of their disruptive behaviour is such that they seriously handicap any examination class. They are also seen as a bad influence on the more vulnerable younger pupils and some of their peers.

In response to serious concerns about discipline in schools a Committee of Enquiry into Discipline in Schools was established by the Secretary of State for Education and Science in March 1988. This was chaired by Lord Elton and the Report produced bears his name (DES, 1989). It was completed at the end of January 1989 and was based on evidence from many sources, mainly mainstream primary and secondary schools, gathered by means of a carefully structured survey of teachers' perceptions of the problem.

From the reports in the press during the mid-1980s about violence and aggression in schools, it was expected that this would be the main worry of teachers in the Elton survey. But this turned out to be not the case. Although, for those who had experienced this, it was a very major problem, for most teachers it was then the day-to-day disruption of classes caused by trivial but persistent misbehaviour which was the main source of concern. However, violence when it did occur was regarded as being very serious.

The Elton Report highlights the need for pupils with emotional and behavioural difficulties to be assessed swiftly so that appropriate intervention can commence. It recognises that, although ideally this should be from support within the school, such a solution is often not realistic because of the level of the acting-out behaviour. Concern was expressed that so much of the alternative provision for the most difficult pupils was improvised as a response to an immediate need. However the need for both on- and off-site units was acknowledged in situations where support within the school was not appropriate.

In these days when schools will be marketing themselves in order to survive, heads are understandably eager not to have their school's reputation undermined by the antics of a few persistent miscreants. In recent years, perhaps it has become easier, and therefore very tempting, to send a year 10 or 11 pupil to the off-side unit than to intervene with special provision within the school. Nevertheless I believe that most schools try hard not to refer too many pupils to special units, and certainly individual teachers often feel a great sense of failure when they have to admit defeat.

The pupils who have been expelled from school form most of the group of pupils with whom I have been concerned during the last 12 years. I hesitate to describe them as maladjusted since some are very well adjusted to their families and communities, and, were the school leaving age still 15, they would probably be well adjusted to working life. Many work in a very efficient and responsible way at their week-end occupations. One of my pupils, Richard, holds down a job as a caretaker of an office block. He has a small flat in the basement and works from 6.00 am until school-time, signs the cleaners in and out between 5.00 pm and 8.00 pm and is responsible for the building during the night.

I have misgivings about this but I do not have the same fears as I had for another boy of the same age and in the same circumstances, both parents divorced and remarried and neither ready or able to offer a home. Billy slept rough 'on the hotplates' (the heating vents on the flat roof of an old people's home on a local council estate) and washed himself and his clothes at school, drying them over the radiators whilst he battled with constant fatigue as he tried to do his school work. At least I know Richard sleeps in a bed at night and has regular meals. If these two boys were still in mainstream school, it is possible that no one would know about their living arrangements.

At their school these boys had been seriously disrupting the classes, which they did not consider relevant to their lives, or simply absenting themselves from class. Although it is easy to empathise with their behaviour, given their circumstances in which they function as adults when out of school, it is impossible to change the school rules to suit the exception. Such is the strength of some adolescents, there may well be youngsters with similar circumstances who, against all odds, are coping with a double life of being a child at school and an adult on the streets outside.

There are two main types of adolescent unit. One is the off-site or on-site unit run by the local authority (Education or Social Services) and offering the best curriculum that can be achieved by three or four teachers in small premises. Most of the pupils in this kind of unit will be there because of their unacceptable acting-out behaviour or their persistent truancy. The other kind is the unit belonging to a hospital psychiatric department. There the emphasis will be on treating the illness, which might involve acting-out behaviour but is as likely to manifest itself in withdrawn behaviour, eating disorders and obsessive behaviours. The head of a psychiatric unit is often a psychiatrist working in partnership with a head of education. In this type of unit teachers have many of the same kinds of problems and experiences as those in the former type but they receive more professional support in coping with the impact that such troubled adolescents can have on those who are trying to teach them.

No unit can provide the facilities, opportunities and stimulus provided by even the smallest high school. What the unit does provide is an opportunity for the adolescents to form a relationship, as individuals, with caring adults and by this means improve their self-image. Because of the very favourable pupil-teacher ratio there is time for each individual to feel respected and listened to. There is also much opportunity for the kind of positive cognitive intervention that is essential for the under-functioning adolescent.

The unit is also an important support for the parents of these adolescents. I am conscious of the fact that we are the 'last resort' and, at the end of the day, when the pupil leaves school for good, it is the parent who will have to find a way of getting him or her to work, and find a way to boost his or her confidence. Often parents do not realise that so much of what they say can be constantly undermining the child. Although I know it is important not to undermine the fragile confidence of an adolescent, I hear myself, in moments of exasperation, saying very cruel and disparaging things to my own teenage sons. Whilst reassuring my pupils' parents that I can understand their problems, I try to help them to see their child's positive achievements and to communicate with their child on occasions when they can offer approval. I ask them to identify the main occasions of contention during the day and explore what can be done about these. Sometimes we are not ready enough to allow a child to learn by the consequences when he or she neglects to perform some duty, such as putting out dirty washing, or budgetting for the weekend.

There is no easy answer to the conflicts between fully-fledged adults and those who are just making the transition. Some of our pupils seem to be more vulnerable than others to criticism and anticipate and react to it before it has even been given. Many demand an impossibly high standard of themselves, often tearing their work up and starting again so many times that nothing is ever completed. Most seem to lack confidence in their own ability and worth.

Perhaps, as teachers of these adolescents who are having a rough ride, our main aim should be to make them believe in themselves. We can only do this if they have tangible achievements in which to believe. Much of the emphasis on documentation about pupils today is about stressing the positive and recognising all successful aspects of a pupils life, not just the conventional academic triumphs. Unfortunately many of our most troubled and troublesome children have to be helped to find the activity in which they can succeed, and even then, their self-esteem is sometimes so low that they have to be persuaded to believe in that success.

CHAPTER 2

Special Units – Educational Topsies

Units in a time of change

The units with which I have had dealings in the last few years are experiencing the ripples, if not the waves, caused by the Education Reform Act (1988). In the first part of this chapter I give an account of five (the names are not the real ones) I visited during 1990, in connection with some research I was undertaking on the place of the preparation for public examinations in units.

I was mainly interested to see to what extent the curriculum in the units was being adapted to cognitively engage and develop the reasoning and intellect of the pupils, or if in fact there was more emphasis on building pupils' self esteem by keeping them occupied with activities in which they had already experienced some measure of success. I also wanted to see whether, overall, a conscious effort was being made to change inappropriate behaviour patterns, or whether the onus was on the staff to be more tolerant of bad behaviours, especially when a pupil was first admitted to the unit.

In the latter part of the chapter, I discuss likely trends in the wake of the Elton Report and recent legislation.

Treetops

Treetops was housed in a collection of single storey prefabricated buildings which had at one time served as local government offices. There were normally 12 pupils on roll, roughly half fourth years and half fifth years, but at the time of my visit, in May, the fifth years had left and the new intake of fourth years would not arrive until September. As is usually the custom in units, staff were known by their first names, although the head had his surname and qualifications on his door. The head had set up this unit six years ago. His previous experience had been in two residential therapeutic communities. He had initially used this model in the unit, but from the start certain modifications had been necessary since the pupils for whom he was now responsible returned to their homes every evening and therefore the continuity of the programme was broken. Regression was a very important part of his programme and pupils were at certain times encouraged to return to infancy and relax among large cushions with cuddly toys. They were allowed to drink from babies' feeding bottles while watching a video in a room full of cushions during the last session of the week. Since the week ended on Thursday this was felt to ease the parting for the long weekend. Troubled children could spend time alone in 'the nest', a tiny room/cupboard equipped with everything one would find in a happy baby's cot.

For the first two years it was left to the choice of the pupils whether they did any 'school-work' or not since counselling was the main activity. However, the head has since felt that the present economic climate makes it necessary to have a curriculum-based programme with the possibility of taking examinations during the final year.

The unit is also involved in the Technical and Vocational Education Initiative Extension (TVEIEX) and the staff are attending meetings to explore the feasibility of preparing pupils for Business and Technology (BTech) Examinations. They already compile their own record of achievement, which pupils receive in a nicely presented folder with the borough's shield. These are carefully prepared and contain external examination certificates as well as internal records. The unit belonged to a cluster group comprising the nearest secondary school and the feeder primaries, and the staff attended regular meetings within this group, mainly about the innovations of the Education Reform Act. They were shortly to receive additional training in preparation for the National Curriculum with a special school group. There is a strong possibility that, within the next year, this unit will be merged with a parallel unit as it would be easier to deliver the National Curriculum with the extended resources afforded by the combined staff teams.

There was a programme of behaviour modification which I actually found disruptive to work, but I realise that the fact I was there and that my visit was on a hot thundery day near the end of the summer term could explain why the pupils acted out. The behaviour modification programme appeared to be based on punishment rather than rewards and worked like this. If a pupil broke any rule he (all three pupils present on that day were boys) was sent 'on to the chair'. This meant he had to leave his seat and sit for a few seconds on a specially provided chair in the corner of the room. If he offended more than three times he would be sent 'on the chair, yogi bear', which meant he had to stay there until told to move. I found it very distracting that the three boys were constantly moving from their seat on to the chair and, in fact, another 'chair' had to be brought into play when two boys were 'on the chair, yogi bear'. One boy was sent into exile as even on the chair he could not behave. This meant he was sent to sit outside the head's room until the head had time to counsel him. Indeed it looked as though the frequency with which the chair was brought into use indicated that the purpose had now been defeated for this group.

During an English lesson I joined in a conversation with the three pupils and their teacher. Since at the time I was doing a survey on examinations in special units I sounded them out on this. One boy, Wayne, insisted that the only thing he wanted to do was mug old grannies and you didn't need exams for this. The second boys, Darren contorted himself into a really small ball and said no one could make him do exams. In contrast, the third boy, Keith, stated an interest in taking exams in maths and computer studies but said he would never do an English exam. He then launched into a discussion with me about what programme I had used to print the questionnaire on exam- inations that I had asked them to complete. He spoke knowledgeably about the merits and demerits of machines that were primarily word processors against those that were computers with a word processing programme.

The teacher then gave the boys the recent AEB paper in English and reminded the aspiring granny mugger that when he had seen fifth years coming out of the exams he had asked to see the paper and said that he could do it easily. The boy agreed that he had said this and that it was so, but he remained adamant that no one was going to con him into doing exams. Darren relaxed from his tightly crouched position and looked at the paper. He then started banging on his desk and saying examinations were 'crap' and so were teachers. This revived the anger in the others.

There is no doubt in my mind that just talking about examinations with these three boys stirred up quite powerful emotions. During part of the time they were too angry to start thinking about putting their feelings on paper. I also thought that they felt some rejection in their placement in the unit. Darren said at one point, 'You don't do exams in a unit'. I contradicted him with the evidence that the fifth years had done so. He replied 'Yes, but no one thinks you can. They think you're a dick-head'. I asked him what made him feel this and he said, 'But they do, don't they?'. I noticed, in his response to the questionnaire, he gave high priority to the statement 'I want to do exams to prove I can do it'. He gave first place to the reason, 'It will help to get me a better job'. Keith gave priority to the statement 'because I know I am better than they think I am'. Wayne recorded the fact that he had no intention of doing exams.

At the end of the day all three boys laid in wait for me around the corner from the unit and asked me if I would like them to accompany me to the station. They were all eager to explain to me why, in their view, things had gone wrong at school and what they thought of the unit. Although they laughed at it as a soft option and obviously found the therapeutic regression quite difficult to understand, they admitted they thought that the teachers there cared for them as people. However they all – even the granny basher – regretted being out of mainstream schools and I sensed quite a loneliness in them. They certainly felt rejected by the system and wished they could go back and try again. I do not know if this time out of school and being with a group of caring adults had given them enough insight into the effect of their behaviour on others to make return to mainstream education a realistic possibility. I was concerned that, because of the method of control used in the unit, I had not had the opportunity to see much continuous work undertaken. I did not feel that the little I saw was cognitively challenging but I realise that I only spent one day there, at the end of the summer term and, without doubt, my presence was in itself a distraction.

I did not feel that the methods used to control behaviour and motivate pupils to work at Treetops could be transferred or modified to use in mainstream education. Although I had grave reservations about the effectiveness of this unit in either educating adolescents or building up their self-esteem. I could not, in one visit, dismiss it as being without educational value.

Riverside

The next establishment visited was an alternative school 30 miles west of London. This had changed out of all recognition since White and Brockington (1978) visited it a decade earlier when it had been a part-time unit run by a voluntary body. It is now a fully constituted school with a Board of Governors. Although it is not a special unit as such I have included it as the clientele are adolescents whose behaviour in mainstream school had been disruptive. At the time of visiting, the fifth year pupils had left and a group of third years had been admitted. Some of these had already spent a year on Home Tuition whilst waiting for a place. The official maximum number on roll is 35, with six full-time teaching staff as well as the head. At the time of my visit there were only 24 on roll as it was a 'low' time of the year. Out of these 14 were present. The head had already found out why the absentees were not there. As I would expect some of the excuses were more believable than others. One mother admitted that her daughter was refusing to leave her bed. She had only started at the school during the previous week and had a long history of school refusal, but she had achieved four attendances in a row during her first week. Another pupil had a dental appointment, and two had 'gone down with something that is going around'. Other apologies included transport problems, a family funeral and an urgent shopping trip. The attendance is generally between 60 and 80 per cent.

First names are used by all. In contrast with Treetops, all six teachers, including the head, were fully involved in the teaching. The third years were taught in one room and the fourth years in another. Those who were reluctant to work and, I think, eager to act out in front of a visitor, were kept on task not with reprimands but with praise and expressions of interest in the small amount of work they had achieved. Even the very quiet, withdrawn members of the group received positive attention without having to seek it and all the children were busy and involved in the work in hand, a clear demonstration of the effectiveness of this positive approach. They were doing maths from an assortment of text books and it was obvious that pupils had been introduced to work that was appropriate to their attainment levels. The rooms were bright and real 'school rooms', with children's work on display and neat posters on the walls.

The head teacher felt strongly that it is better for the pupils to apply for jobs with no examinations than to have results which label them as low achievers. She identified lack of self-esteem as the main factor causing the inability to be educated in mainstream schools, and felt that self-esteem could only be built up by providing a curriculum which would ensure that all pupils had maximum opportunity of success without any risk of failure or rejection. Although she did not speak about cognitive intervention and developing the pupils' ability for reasoning and exploring, the teaching was of such a quality that these were taking place all the time.

Some of the staff were not so sure about the justification for having no examinations. The head admitted that it was quite hard to stand out against the pressure for examinations from parents and pupils as it was becoming increasingly difficult to prove to the outside world that these pupils were achieving. She was quite fearful about the effect the National Curriculum and compulsory testing will have on the school, and was adamant that she wanted 'disapplication' from the National Curriculum.

When I spoke to the pupils I did not give them the questionnaire as there was no possibility of their taking examinations. Instead I talked to them generally about the problem and they seemed to really enjoy being asked their opinions. One boy of Pakistani origin (a fairly recent immigrant) said his father, uncles and cousins were very worried that he would not be doing examinations. He hoped he would be able, nevertheless, to go to college after he left, but he still found it difficult to face coming to the alternative school every day.

I was impressed with the head's sincerity and strength in holding out against examination work. The atmosphere in the school was gentle and nurturing and there seemed to be not only a genuine caring between pupils and staff but also valuable intellectual development.

Ferndown

The third unit I visited is in a neighbouring London borough. It is based on the first floor of an old high school which is now used as a teachers' centre and for adult education. It has four classrooms, a craft room, an office and a staff room plus lavatories for the use of pupils and teachers at the unit. It takes 24 children from age 10 up to 16. As in most units the great majority of the pupils are in their last two years of schooling and in general the children are there because they act out too much to be contained in their mainstream classrooms. Unlike the other two units it is the intention to help as many as possible to go back into mainstream school, especially the younger pupils. If the very young ones cannot be returned to mainstream they will be state-mented for attendance at a more suitable school. For the purpose of my visit, however, I was concerned only with those in the top class, most of whom were already in their final year.

The head teacher was about to retire after 20 years in this unit. She made use of the range of facilities available for these children, including alternative examinations, in which they could find some success. In contrast to Riverside the curriculum was individually planned to give the pupils as many qualifications as possible by the time they left.

I felt that this unit had retained many of the advantages of a small school because the head had been so efficient in securing examination resources for her pupils, while also having all the advantages of the specially favourable pupil-teacher ratio afforded in a unit. Unusually for a small unit, there were five computers in a special room, and a teacher who was competent to lead the children in this study. Here and elsewhere I felt there was very worthwhile cognitive intervention of the kind that is possible when there are only six pupils to each teacher.

Because the pupils had seen me visit their head on other occasions they carried on much as normal. There were the usual altercations which are part and parcel of dealing with challenging pupils in the classroom but there was a business-like atmosphere all the same. I felt that it was a wise and sensitive move to give the 14-to-16 year-olds a different recreation time from the others because of the different priorities of this group. However much one deplores the preoccupation with smoking and discussing the sexual and illicit activities of the previous evening among this group, it has to be accepted as inherent to the stage of development. However, as teachers *in loco parentis*, we have a duty to protect younger pupils from being led into bad habits whilst in our care.

Lavender Street

My next unit was an Intermediate Treatment Unit with twelve pupils and six staff of whom the principal and three others are social workers. Because it is an IT unit there is also an evening young offenders' project to which some staff are committed during evening sessions. The principal and the head of education share responsibility for the evening session, with help from at least one of the social workers. The social workers, once they have visited the homes of absentees, also share fully in the teaching activity, Each child has a key worker who might be a social worker or a teacher.

The emphasis in this unit is very much on social and life skills. Nevertheless, because the pupils requested it, they now enter for the same examinations as our students in Orchard View and achieve similar results. I feel this group has done well in these examinations because it was their idea to do them, and the fact that the staff team was at first hesitant has made the pupils more determined to do well.

Sparkwell

This unit has grown out of the overloading of the Home Tuition Service with requests for tuition for pupils in their final year of school.

It is housed in one of the ubiquitous prefabricated huts used for other fringe support services on the same site. These include a Youth Training Scheme for slow learners, Adult Literacy provision, and a drop-in Law Centre. It was approached up a narrow street, lined with warehouses, and situated in a triangle between the railway and the main road. In this unit there are 28 pupils on roll and eight teachers, as well as the headteacher who is the only person there full-time. All the pupils and the assistant teachers are there for a specified number of sessions. Pupils are rarely in the same group more than twice in a week. Some of the pupils spend very little time on this site as they attend courses at the local FE College, and a few go back to their schools for certain lessons.

I was impressed by the quiet, business-like atmosphere, and the industry of the pupils. The head knew each pupil well and was able to tell me about the individual programme each one was following. Attendance was high (around 90 per cent) but if any of the pupils missed their sessions the head contacted the education welfare office immediately. Some pupils were attached to social workers with whom the head liaised, but her main role was in making sure each pupil had an appropriate programme to follow. Two of the teachers were specialists in specific learning difficulties.

There was no feeling of belonging to this unit. You came, you did your work, you were entered for your examinations, you took them and you collected your certificates. Because the programmes of work were suitably differentiated, the pupils were, without exception, very positive about how much better they had achieved since being there. As usual most said that they regretted not being able to complete their education in mainstream school but they felt that the teachers at the unit had helped them, and the head knew how to get the best for them. Although I am sure it was not a well thought out policy for the pupils to lack identity with the unit, I think this was one of its strengths.

Orchard View

I finish my account of units with a brief description of the one that I ran for 12 and a half years. The main difference between Orchard View and the other units was that it accommodated only those children who were in the final term of year 10 or in year 11. This decision had been taken because of the difficulty in returning pupils to school. With only those in their final year it was possible to plan that year when pupils could be supported on work experience, counselled on possible careers and helped to gain examination certificates.

The curriculum of the unit evolved continuously as staff became aware of initiatives that were working in other schools or units. Each year programmes that motivated pupils and increased their self-esteem were adopted. Other programmes that were tried but failed to engage pupils were abandoned after a fair trial. Although in units there is often emphasis on the importance of achieving good social relationships in order to enable behaviourally disordered children to learn, we found that it was often a satisfying, successful experience of learning that enabled our youngsters to begin to relate to us. Individual counselling in response to a need identified by the child was an important feature. Unlike other support services, we saw the same pupils everyday, so we could wait for the child to feel ready to respond and in this way we supported individual pupils through a number of crises. Because of regular links with the child care planning officer we were able to obtain prompt help for children, and support for ourselves, from social services.

The curriculum was 'in the spirit of the National Curriculum'. Although hampered by the small number of staff we tried to cover appropriate objectives and developed assignments, at differentiated levels of difficulty, across the curriculum. During this last year of our pupils' compulsory education we introduced them to well known literature, music and art, an effort in which we were well rewarded. Nevertheless, since the aim of the unit was to ensure that every pupil left to go into a job, on to a training course or to further education, personal and social education was a high priority. Work experience was arranged for those who requested it and had shown us a reasonable degree of commitment to keeping appointments.

Because the unit was situated close to the High Street we had a continuous stream of ex-pupils visiting. Although this was not always convenient we were always pleased when they 'lectured' current pupils on the importance of working hard and doing what the staff told them. They were also helpful in finding jobs for a number of our leavers.

Units and their public image

However carefully we try to run a unit which is purposeful and effective, we cannot avoid the reputation of units as 'sin bins'. For this reason, several years ago, I made the decision not to have the name of my unit on examination certificates. In general, I have serious doubts about placing all the most disruptive and disaffected youngsters in the area under the same roof. I am even more concerned about the feeling that they should want a corporate identity. To wish to be identified with an institution which is known to be for pupils who have been unable to finish their education in mainstream, could indicate a resignation to being outside the normal hopes and aspirations of the peer group. This could indicate the kind of poor self-image that leads some adults to constantly re-offend in order to be returned to custody, and others to remain unemployed because of failure to conform to the demands of paid employment. I feel that it is a healthy attitude to see the unit as a 'crutch' or 'haven' that was available when needed but was a process passed through in order to attain a successful passage to adult life.

As authorities have more commitment to keeping difficult youngsters within mainstream education by means of teams of Outreach workers, it is important that practice in successful units is looked at to see if it could be adapted for use in mainstream. Many of the methods of engaging pupils in the units are only possible because of the small numbers and the off-site situation. However, some of the positive reinforcement of good behaviour, the attention to individual needs and the quiet courtesy between teacher and taught, which often has to start with the teacher giving some leeway at first, can be used in a setting with a less favourable pupil:teacher ratio.

One of the problems that seems to be common with most of the pupils, and many of their parents, is their lack of commitment to anything outside themselves and their own families. I think one of the reasons why Sparkwell is so successful for its pupils is that they are not expected to commit themselves further than attending the classes for which they are timetabled. The teachers have only realistic hopes for them and therefore there is no disappointment to hand on to the pupils. There is a wholly positive ethos in a unit where there are 'tailor made' differentiated aims for each individual pupil.

Pupils are only transferred from a mainstream school after very careful consideration. It is seen very much as a last resort and at the time of the actual transfer the pupil might display a certain amount of bravado. However, within weeks many realise that they have placed themselves outside their peer group. There are feelings of rejection and failure, and misgivings about the effect their placement in a 'sin bin' will have on their applications for jobs when they leave school. I would be concerned for the young person who wanted to carry his or her identity as a member of this group beyond the experimental years of adolescence.

There is, of course, a danger, especially if the unit is the focus of unfortunate publicity, that a certain group of young people might take a pride in their identity as a member of an educational establishment which is considered to be outside the normal system. Few would dispute that these pupils have problems that require addressing if they are to pass from the world of school to that of the young worker. The unit might well be able to help one or two of these young people at a time but, if the majority have this attitude, then the value will be lost for other, more vulnerable pupils. The balance of the needs of the students in any unit has to receive careful consideration if the unit is not to become a 'sin-bin' or a dumping ground whose only function is to keep certain pupils out of the classroom and away from their peers. Other strategies, which will be discussed fully in the final chapter, are being looked at to prevent a 'unit sub-culture' from expanding.

The Elton Report

The Elton Report (DES, 1989) contained 138 recommendations for action in schools to improve behaviour and to create orderly conditions in which pupils can learn. Among the recommendations were:

> the need for the rapid assessment of the special educational needs of pupils with emotional and behavioural difficulties . . . LEAs to ensure that failure to identify and meet the learning needs of some pupils is not the cause of their bad behaviour (p. 15).

It is noted that,

> while all LEAs make alternative provision for the most difficult pupils, its pattern tends to be more or less improvised response to needs and difficulties (p. 153).

There is an acknowledged need for LEAs to review their alternative provision, noting that although support should be given to pupils and teachers in schools, there may also be a need for off-site units, at least for short-term admissions.

Among the effects that the 1988 Education Reform Act is having on units is the question of who will pay for them under Local Management of Schools (LMS). There is also concern about whether pupils in units will receive the National Curriculum to which this Act entitles them since what pupils are taught in alternative units is

24

governed by the staff who are available. Additionally, in the usual eccentric accommodation available, there is a lack of suitable space for practical work and equipment.

It is clear that the 1990s will be the decade when units will be fighting for survival, and in many cases will be forced into surrender. Certainly they will have to be much more accountable to the outside world, and willing to evaluate what they are doing, and to be evaluated.

CHAPTER 3

The Pupils in the Units

I have lost count of the times I have been asked to describe a 'typical pupil' in the unit. There is no such pupil. However, when teachers from units get together we are always amazed at the similarities we find between our pupils. In the course of doing my research on preparing pupils in units for examinations, I was interested to find that there was a very high rate of similarity between the answers given by pupils and in teachers' responses from all over the country. It was also interesting that, if the pupil responses were accurate, the teachers did not have the same eagerness as the pupils for attempting some examinations. Nor did the teachers' perceptions of the reasons for pupils wanting to do examinations tally with the pupils' declared reasons. Many of the teachers were afraid that the pupils would not feel able to take the risk of failure, and rejected the idea of pupils seeing examinations as a challenge. On the other hand, the pupils declared themselves eager to 'have a go', and one of the main reasons for attempting exams was 'to prove that I am better than they think I am'. In Chapter 6 I shall be discussing examinations in more detail.

When describing pupils in units I can only give an account of those I have encountered in my South London borough. Since the ratio of boys to girls in the unit is approximately 3:2, I shall use the masculine pronoun when referring to pupils.

Education and family tradition

Some of these pupils came from families where there has never been a tradition of valuing education. Often parents have introduced themselves by saying how they always hated school too, though they often go on to defend their position by pointing out how well they have done since. It is not unusual for these parents to run successful businesses and drive up-market cars. They work hard and they play hard, and I have a gut feeling that the child before me will have little difficulty in making his or her way in the world once the statutory obligation to attend school is discharged. With these parents I talk about the necessity to obey the law of the land. They listen to me with amused but polite tolerance when I extol the virtues of education and the gaining of a couple of examination certificates. I know that they will ensure the child attends the unit just enough to keep the Education Welfare Officer off their backs because they do not want to waste time going to court near the end of their child's school life. When they ring up and say that 'He's not too well today but will probably be in tomorrow', I try to sound slightly concerned but not totally conned as I know this is probably 'parent-speak' for 'we are extra busy and we need his extra pair of hands at our disposal today'.

Youngest in the family

A child with similar reasons for losing interest in school is the one who is the youngest of a family where everyone else is working. Whilst truanting or suspended he has probably been earning a bit on the side by going to work with one of the older siblings. Again the parents will encourage their offspring to come to the unit as they do not want the bother of a court appearance when the child will soon be leaving anyway. They will tell me of various members of the family who have been allowed to leave school early, explaining that they can get 'work experience' for their child. They argue with me when I explain the rules by which I can sanction work experience and I know that the pupil will have absences which will be excused in terms of 'after an Indian take-away' or 'something that's going round', and he will return sun-tanned and with calloused hands. The pupil has probably grown out of what we are trying to offer as education. Both these categories of pupil demonstrate the need for vocational education after the age of 14. My worry for them on personal grounds is that they are often working uninsured in very unsuitable conditions. Those who are helping out in the family business will be looked after by their parents, but those doing casual jobs are wide open to exploitation by employers who will pay cash in hand below the going rate, and probably employ them for work unsuitable for a youth under 18.

The common factor in both these cases is that the parents either see nothing wrong in lying to authority, or genuinely think they will be believed. Either way the pupil has difficulties with fitting in with our idea of being truthful within the small community of the unit. I was gratified that one boy, Laurence, did have the grace to seem embarrassed when he was caught out recently. His father runs a firm of contractors who frequently do odd maintenance jobs in Inner London schools. One morning he rang me very early to say Laurence had been 'bringing his guts up all night' and the health department really ought to do something about the local Indian take-away. The son was taken by surprise when, wielding his father's paintbrush in the corridor of a Junior School, he was spotted by his teacher from the unit who was there that morning being interviewed for a vacancy.

These pupils are difficult to motivate to do school work, especially in the case of those who are already useful in the family firm, as they know they are going to have no difficulty finding employment. They have little vested interest in examination success since their role models have usually managed without certificates from school.

In the case of some of the youngest children of families, who start casual work before they leave school, it is evident that the working siblings feel threatened by the likelihood of the youngest passing examinations, and actually positively discourage it. However, in one case where this was happening we managed to involve the older brother in his younger brother's work. We used the fortuitous imminence of a court appearance and the accompanying court report as an excuse to encourage the younger boy to do his best. In the end both brothers were entered for the examination and the older one was as pleased as the younger one when he found out he had passed with distinction. This shows that the pupils at these units are not necessarily without academic ability.

Parent and pupil victims

We do not have the same feeling of optimism about employment in relation to all the young people who are referred to us. Often they are accompanied by a depressed, unemployed parent. The story they tell us is a familiar one. Teachers are reported to have always had a down on their child. There is a catalogue of petty injustices at school about homework, make-up, hair (or lack of!), detentions, lost property and taking the blame for everyone else. I am not surprised to hear that the parent had the same trouble her/himself. In fact there is often a serious dispute with neighbours going on right now. I often learn that I have already had one or more members of the same extended family and, although I can remember all these pupils blaming me for all their ills and constantly telling me that what I had to offer was 'crap', I am now told how much they loved being at Orchard View and how they have said it will be the solution to all their problems if only I will accept their child as a pupil.

In one particular case I remember a mother told me, outside court, that her son would never have been in trouble for dishonest handling of goods were it not for me. She said she hoped I would lose my job and be as unhappy as she was. She rang me almost a year later and again harangued me over my (imagined) part in having her son jailed for dealing in pornography. This second charge was 11 months after he had left school. Yet here she was now, supporting her sister in pleadng for a place for her nephew. She reckoned her son would never have done so well in the prison classes had he not had such a good education at Orchard View!

One of the most difficult aspects of my work is working daily with people who are pulling me in to play a part in their double act. In my first few years I became hurt and angry at the accusations of parents, and then their assumption that I would have forgotten all the animosity by the time they were next in need of my services. I now have the experience to recognise the recriminations as the parent's need to find someone safe to blame. I also have the confidence to face them with what has gone before and help them to recognise what they are doing. I hope this is helpful to them. Even if they are unable to learn from this, it is quite important for my own self-esteem that they do not feel that I am willing to act as their verbal 'punch-bag'. I know that once pupils are referred to me I have to accept them as this is the 'end of the line', but I have to try to bluff each one into thinking that they have passed through the interview by their own skill in impressing me.

The cuckoo in the nest

The parents I feel sorry for are those lone mothers who have lost control over their adolescent off-spring. They resemble particularly vulnerable small birds being terrorised by large cuckoos. As I interview the child I can see the mother, nervous of putting a step wrong as her outrageous off-spring lounges in the chair and tries to look as tough and as bored as possible. I know that it will be up to us to support the mother and give her confidence rather than expect her to support the 'cuckoo' in his or her attendance with us. I use 'her' here as more female than male cuckoos come to us. It is easy to believe that this mother has given up and it is her own fault that the relationship has reached this stage. Often this mother has suffered more than I could ever bear at the hands of one or more brutal partners and, if she has been a very young mother, she might have also suffered from the smothering possessiveness of her parents when the 'cuckoo' was a baby. We are usually told what sweet babies our cuckoos were, and how they could wind everyone round their little finger.

We did have one cuckoo with two tiny parents. As a child, the wife had been physically and sexually abused by her father and now felt worth nothing. The husband had always been small and had been overprotected by his family to such an extent that at one time he had been persuaded to go home to live and go through a 'mock' separation from his wife so that they could increase their income with single parent allowance. However they were a loving couple and had got back together but their two boys saw them as being very weak. We realised that one boy, David, only attended because his parents bought him a computer game every time he came to us. They were too frightened of incurring their son's displeasure not to, but even more scared of being taken to court for the boy's non-attendance at school. I put the responsibility for this firmly on the son's shoulders and set up a meeting where this message could be spelt out by a multi-disciplinary team. The Children's Act (1990), while admirable in most respects, will remove the threat of care for non-attendance at school, a matter which has so far kept this boy and his younger brother in line with the law on absenteeism.

Another of my cuckoos is a large red-headed girl called Linda. Her mother is a slightly faded, but very cowed, version of herself. When she came for the interview the girl had just been shopping with her mother and entered with a family size packet of Mars bars in her hand. She proceeded to eat her way through the first two and was about to unwrap a third when I said, 'No, that's enough, Linda'. Her mother looked terrified, and I realised that she was afraid of what this monstrous girl would do when crossed. I had heard of the Child Care Planning Meeting where she had had a full blown tantrum in front of a panel of social workers, a psychologist, the head of year, the Educational Welfare Officer and her formidable granny, with whom she and her mother live. Apparently only granny could stop her, by threatening to slap her. When her mother had refused to give her pocket money as there was concern about her spending the money on drink, the girl had persuaded a neighbour to lend her large sums which the mother subsequently had to repay.

When Linda joined us she would make frequent inappropriate demands. One afternoon she had a sore throat so she demanded I should give her a lozenge or an antibiotic. I explained to her that this was not my role. It was very fortunate that I had accidently left the video camera in my room and was able to use it quickly. Only she and I watched the video as I had no wish to humiliate her. Linda was not amused at seeing herself, stamping her foot and screwing up her face as I calmly refused to give in. She was interested when I spoke to her about the part of us that is always a child and how, in order to be treated as adults, we have to make sure that we do not use this part of ourselves to get our own way. She agreed that she would not want her boyfriend to see her having a tantrum (she did not actually have a boyfriend at the time). She pleaded with me not to ever let her granny or mother see the video. I pointed out that this would not be necessary as they often saw the real thing! At this she buried her head in her hands. I understand there have been few subsequent tantrums at home.

Bereaved children

Each year, out of an average of 20 boys, we have at least three who have lost their father. Usually we have one or two of our dozen girls who have lost a mother or a father. It is interesting that it is the death of a father that seems to cause a boy to disaffect most. However, we often learn about the early loss of a mother by chance since a large number of fathers have remarried and it is the step-mother who comes to the interview with the child, without necessarily mentioning that she is the step-mother. I feel that the single parent family which has become that way through bereavement presents very different problems from the ones created by divorce, separation or the mother remaining unmarried. Whereas there is not the conflict of loyalties and open bitterness towards the non-custodial parent that is usually expressed by divorced and separated parents, there is an unacknowledged anger with the deceased which neither the pupil nor the surviving parent has put into words. It is the pain of being left to cope with life without that loved person. Very often the parent is surprised when I ask about the deceased parent at the interview, and I am told the pupil 'took it very well', 'didn't seem to take much notice' or 'we never talked about it'. At this point the pupil often looks away or I see his eyes fill with tears. There is obviously a great deal of unresolved sorrow and anger in many of our pupils and the single parent has had little help with coping with this. In fact she is often still needing support herself at a time when her adolescent needs even more support than others of the same age. This is a case when it is easy to blame the moodiness and unpredictability of adolescence for problems which in a younger or older person would be seen to originate from grief, and would gain sympathy rather than censure.

We have had a few pupils whose parents have either died by their own hands, or in some violent way. In these cases the children have faced the additional burden of keeping a secret if they have come from a different area. They might also have had to cope with the disruption of media interest at the time of the tragedy.

At one time I had two girls from the same family. Their mother presented herself as a very capable, sensible woman who had dealt well with her husband's sudden death whilst the girls were toddlers. She received much support from the older girl who had been 8 at the time. They were more like sisters, or even like a husband and wife when they attended child care planning meetings together. The middle girl was very quiet and meek, a low-achiever at everything except art, a subject in which she was extremely gifted and expressive. The youngest girl was always thought to be older than her sister. She was noisy, outspoken and would have been a high achiever had she attended school regularly and had the 'right' attitude. She confided in me that she felt she would like to get in touch with her father's family who lived in the north of England and asked me how she could find out the address. When I asked why she could not just ask her mother, an incredible story came out about how the father had been killed outside a pub, probably by a contract killer, and if the family knew where her mother was they would almost certainly put the police on to her. As a very little girl, she said she could remember being taken by her mother to visit the man in prison who had killed her dad.

I do not know whether this story was true or not. I do believe that the girls believed it and felt the whole family to be under some threat from the outside world. Whatever the truth of the matter I am sure the events surrounding the father's death were responsible for the fact that both girls wasted their educational opportunities.

Another case of bereavement concerns a boy called Dean, whose father had died in a motor-cycle accident. His mother was at her wit's end as this boy's behaviour was so erratic and, at times, aggressive. She said he had never even mentioned his father after he had died when Dean was 12. There was rarely a day in school when Dean did not tell us about how clever his father was and how he still had his tools, which he took a pride in using to carry out little jobs around the house and garden. He took a pride in doing a repair before his mother even noticed that it was needed. I think he would have found it impossible to settle to work even in our sympathetic setting, had he not been able to share his thoughts about his father with us. When I mentioned this to his mother she said 'He's only doing it for sympathy and show', and then burst into tears and said, 'Its alright for him. No one thinks about me. He thinks if he does what his father would have done, I won't miss him, but I do'. Before we could do much for Dean educationally we had to help his mother to praise him and help the boy not to walk away from his mother's tears.

The families of many of our pupils have collapsed in some way, whether by death or divorce or separation. I often feel that one of the functions of the staff at the unit is to form a united family that is strong enough to withstand the hostility and disappointment which some of our pupils need to express. It is also important that we can help them to understand why they feel angry and despairing at times.

At school some of our pupils have given vent to feelings that their own families are too fragile to weather. At first the staff have tried to be understanding because they know something of the child's difficulties at home, but there is a limit to how much acting-out behaviour any mainstream school can contain.

Children who 'parent' the family

Sometimes when a parent bends under the pain and pressure of loss, a child becomes strong enough to cope with many of the practical needs of the family, especially caring for the younger children. Some of our pupils have attended case conferences on younger members of the family on behalf of the parent(s). Many have been responsible for making sure their younger siblings have uniform ready for school, and they are the ones who write the absence notes and the PE excuse notes. A number of adults outside the family recognise and respect the adult role that the child has taken on. Few, however, recognise the anomaly of then treating the 'parent' child as a child in school, and expecting the same meek compliance to rules. There are additional contradictions when the child who is parenting a family is also in an adult sexual relationship.

Maria was an example of this situation. Both her parents were of low intelligence and very disorganised in managing the family budget. Maria had one older brother and six younger brothers and sisters. The older four children had attended special boarding schools for much of their education, but by the time the younger two reached school age the Warnock Report had been published and very few pupils were being sent out of the borough to a special school. Both children were therefore placed at the local primary school where they received much support from the Educational Welfare Service and a social worker who had been attached to the family since the birth of the first child. Kenny, the eldest brother, came to us when he started to abscond from his boarding school. It was thought that a year in the unit would be good preparation for him before he started to look for a job in his own locality. When Kenny left the boarding school Maria demanded to do the same and, as she was a girl of average intelligence who had shone amongst the other pupils at her special school, it was decided to place her at a sympathetic local secondary school.

The eldest two children being at home put considerable strain on the accommodation in their small house, and even more on the finances. At this time the father was before the court, yet again, on a long string of charges including more unpaid fines and missed sessions of community service than could be dealt with without a custodial sentence. Mother was left on her own with the children at a time when her two eldest were, for the first time since they were very little, living permanently at home, and she was having to send the two youngest to an ordinary school. This coincided with the retirement of the social worker who had supported her for 16 years.

The mother coped with some of the financial problems by taking a lodger, who before long was sharing Maria's bed; but, as Kenny said, it was OK because they were engaged! Mother accepted the fact meekly when Maria and the lodger took over parenting the rest of the family. Teachers at the little ones' school commented on the improvement in standards of cleanliness and uniform now that Maria was in charge. Maria had, after all, had the benefits of an aspiring middle-class boarding education that mother had lacked. She even took it upon herself to visit me to check on Kenny's progress at school. She was very indignant when her own school wrote to her mother about her absences, and she told her mother to ignore the letters. When the Educational Welfare Service managed to return her to school she was truculent and took on the teachers whenever she felt they were 'victimising' another child.

Soon after this a younger sister was transferred from her boarding school to the same school as Maria, as part of the post-Warnock programme of reintegration. There were terrible problems if ever Maria thought any teacher was at all 'out of order' with her sister Jeannie (although she felt entitled to thump the living daylights out of her for the slightest peccadillo). This culminated one day in Maria marching into a classroom and physically attacking a teacher. She was suspended and sent to us.

I feel this train of events was inevitable from the time Maria took over as the parent in the family. We had tremendous difficulties with managing her as she seemed like an adult to us in many ways, and yet eventually she was able to show us her vulnerable side. We were able to support her on the day she went home and found her mother in bed with the same lodger Maria had slept with. We spent many hours helping her to understand how roles in her family had been switched and making her feel that it was OK for her to express the needs of a teenager and to reject some of the burden of responsibility she was taking for others until she could feel more responsible for herself.

There are other ways in which we have seen children take an almost parental responsibility for their own parent. Sam was the youngest child of a mother who had been divorced by two husbands and widowed by her third. I had already had a nephew of Sam's in the unit two years before as Sam had been born when his eldest sister already had two children. There was always confusion in my mind over who were siblings and who were of the next generation. At home there was just Sam and an elderly, very depressed mother. She had repeatedly kept Sam out of school for company ever since his older siblings had left home. There was a long history of all seven children in the family having poor school attendance. During each time of family crisis mum had kept one of them at home with her. Over the years she had become more and more reluctant to leave the house and had insisted on having someone with her in case she needed something from the shop. This was diagnosed as part of her depression rather than agoraphobia since she was able to go out to the pub and bingo after the school day had ended.

The authority took the mother to court over Sam's repeated absence from school and he was placed in care. He became extremely anxious and referred constantly to his mother. On the first two occasions when he went home it was to find her unconscious, having just taken an overdose. Fortunately she recovered completely after prompt intervention. This pattern of events only stopped after the social worker realised how carefully the overdose was timed, for on one occasion she arrived at the house a short interval before Sam was due home and found her with pills but not having taken them. Sam did not begin to succeed in school learning until he was allowed to return home to live. We managed to help him maintain reasonable attendance by making his mum welcome to drop in and see us at lunch time. Social Services worked very carefully with this family and there was outpatient help from the psychiatric wing of the local hospital. I have since had two of Sam's nieces, both of whom had truanted repeatedly and both of whom had been found by EWOs at the grandmother's house when truanting.

At present I have a girl, Susie, who is looking after her father into whose custody she was placed after the break up of her parent's marriage. I did not know the situation until the afternoon when Susie demanded to be allowed to use my phone. I always remain present when my phone is being used, a situation with which Susie was not at all happy. She was anxiously ringing her grandmother to find out whether they had seen her father during the last two days. Apparently he had lost his job and, because he was depressed, she suspected he had been out drinking. She then went on to tell me about her father's drink problem and the effect on their lives. She told me that he had had so many debts that all the furniture had been sold and they now had only their mattresses and bedding. When I expressed my concern that Susie was going back to such a bleak place on her own, she sought to allay my fears by telling me that she stays in the pub until it closes and someone usually buys her a pie or a sandwich. I asked if she could eat with her mother's family who live very near the unit. She explained that she is not welcome there since she always causes trouble with her younger siblings.

Is it surprising, in these circumstances, that Susie finds it impossible to accept the child's role she is expected to play at school? At the age when an adolescent most needs to be secure enough in her relationship with her parents to be able to be looking optimistically towards the natural stage of independence from them, she is out looking for her dad.

Keeping the family secret

One very worrying kind of pupil is the one that is very difficult to define as it is often some years after the child has passed through the unit that we have any idea about what train of events could have led up to this pupil becoming disruptive or disaffected. This is the pupil who comes from a home where there is a family secret. In saying this, I am not suggesting that I am entitled to be privy to any family's secrets. Heaven forbid! The problem here is that there is a secret that some members of the family know and others do not. For example, I have had cases where the child knew that another child in the same class at school had the same father as her but she knew that her mother was not aware of this. Where there have been secrets the family has often presented as a secure and fairly prosperous unit, with one or both parents in professional or skilled employment. The parents appear to be totally baffled by the difficulties of the referred child and are desperately trying to hang the blame on some outside agency.

Although some family secrets only come to light after many years, and I am sure there are some we never discover, some come out when I am counselling either the child or the parent, or working with the whole family. In one case it transpired that the father had served a prison sentence in connection with a warehouse theft when the two boys in the family were toddlers. The mother had worked hard at making sure that the boys never found out. They had moved on many occasions in the previous 12 years since each time someone who had known them during this period crossed their path, they would move on to another district, leaving no forwarding address. They were devastated when the younger boy, Ronnie, was in court on a number of theft charges. At this time I did not know the dad's history and I was concerned at the anguish of the mother. It was Ronnie who first told me with some anger that his parents did not know, and he could never tell them, that he knew about his father's past, and why should they be so surprised at his deeds in the circumstances? It was decided that I should prepare Ronnie to tell his parents what he knew whilst I was there to support him. When the news was broken the father seemed totally unsurprised and relieved that the facts were out in the open. Although the mother sobbed and said she would be too ashamed to ever face me again, she came and spoke to me very calmly the next day and all the family were able to focus more constructively on Ronnie's problems.

In a similar case the parents were devastated by the delinquency of their son who had been in and out of the juvenile court since an early age. During the course of a meeting with them the mother admitted that she had always tried to give everything she could to the boy because before she had him she had had a baby whom she placed for adoption. For this she had never forgiven herself so she had lavished the love for both children on her first legitimate child, but he had been very jealous when two younger children were born some time later. Bob's delinquency coincided with the next child starting school.

June was another one with a family secret. She was an attractive redhead, whose main offence at school was impertinence.

Unfortunately she answered back the deputy head in front of some of the younger girls and, in the circumstances she had to go. She was a girl of average ability who produced good neat work. Unfortunately she rarely finished anything and often tore up her best work as soon as she had finished it. I felt that she was determined not to succeed in anything. If I complimented her, she was either abusive or asked me if I fancied her. One day she asked if she could talk to me at break time. She sat and told me, in a monotone, that her brother was sexually abusing her every night whilst her mother was at work. She said this had been going on for a considerable period. I talked to her for some time after break and, to give her time to sleep on it, I spoke to her again the next day and told her that we would have to involve the police because the law had been broken. I explained that this was not uncommon and there was a procedure we had to follow. She agreed, and the wheels were set in motion. But when the police came and the girl had to speak in the presence of her mother, she said I had made it all up. She swore there was no truth in the sexual abuse at all and I had suggested it to her to stop her mother from working. The police reprimanded me for wasting their time and departed. It was six years later, just after her divorce from a rich man, 30 years her senior whom she had married three weeks after leaving school, when she came into my office to talk. She said her original stories were true. She apologised for lying to the police and told me that she had been having therapy for 18 months to try to get over the abuse. She felt that this had been the cause of the break-up of their marriage as her husband could not forgive her for letting herself be abused.

Adopted children

There is another very tiny group of children who, I think, are in a separate category. They are the few pupils we have had who have known that they are adopted. I qualify this as, if they do not know they are adopted, the chances are that I will not either. I have become aware, over a number of years of involvement with families, how often children in families are adopted and never know that their sister, aunt or cousin is in fact their mother. I think I have taken a great interest in the four adopted children who have attended the unit since, as the adoptive mother of three grown sons, I do realise that knowledge of adoption is often much harder to bear than it appears to the outside world. I also realise how much parents have invested in making it seem as if everything is going according to plan.

In three of the four cases, the schools spoke very highly of the parents and stated that they could not understand why they were having such problems with their child since they were all parents who valued education and supported the school. The parents who were not so well regarded were working class and lived on a large council estate. All the others were middle class, living in the leafy avenues, and each parent had professional qualifications.

Delia, the first child in this situation to come to my notice, had been adopted in infancy, like her brother who was two years older; they had been adopted from a religious adoption society as her parents were regular church-goers. She had been to an independent school until she passed the 11-plus which enabled her to attend a very popular selective school in the public sector. She had done well there during the first three years, but in the fourth year she had acquired a boyfriend with a criminal reputation and had started 'bunking off' during school days and doing no homework. She also engineered her suspension by breaking the strict uniform rules. Delia's parents tried to dissuade her from her choice of boyfriend but later, having admitted defeat, made him welcome at their home and tried to meet his parents. They tried in other ways to give Delia more freedom whilst still remaining in control.

The parents also allowed Delia to transfer to a comprehensive school where she said she would be happy. It was much larger than her former school and for several weeks she managed to attend for registration but leave shortly afterwards. It was her mother who saw her in town and alerted the school. Even on days when her mother took her right into the form room, Delia had absconded by 9.30 am.

The parents were upset when she was referred to us. After a false start on the first day, she settled down and came regularly but became firmly attached to the criminal element in the group, spoke with a broad south London accent and swore frequently. It was then becoming obvious that Delia was pregnant. All the same she said she would like to do her O Levels (this was in 1983) and we went to great lengths to get the books and give her special lessons. She did not work at all however and by March was found, despite vehement denials, to be eight months pregnant. She came back after the birth because she was bored, and showed no emotion when the baby was taken into care and placed for adoption. She visited me recently, relating how she is now a reformed character: she now runs a record company, is married to a luxury car dealer, has two sons who are being privately educated and she loves to spend Sundays with her parents.

In many ways, Caroline had a very similar set of circumstances. She was adopted by a religious family with a son seven years older than her. Both her parents were ministers in their evangelical church and Caroline had conformed completely with their idea of a good daughter until puberty. She had become pregnant shortly after her fourteenth birthday. She admitted that she did not know who the father was, as she had had sex with a number of boys at the time when conception had taken place. After much heart-searching by the whole family the decision had been made to have the pregnancy terminated. When I first met the family there was still a great deal of guilt about this abortion in evidence. She had been referred to the unit because she had been truanting from school. The school was very shocked at her promiscuity as she still presented as a very good little girl with her immaculate uniform, short socks and shining hair in a very conservative style.

After she started with us she was very unself-conscious in handing out leaflets to encourage the other pupils to join the church youth club. She still attended Sunday School and tried to interest others in meeting her there and giving it a try. She told them the singing was 'really inspirational'. I was surprised that she was such a heavy smoker, and even more surprised when she confided in me within weeks of coming to us that she was again pregnant and intended to keep the baby. It was decided that I would invite her parents in and I would be there when she told them. Such was the communication and care between Caroline and her mother, that she could not keep the news of the pregnancy to herself until the appointment we had made and she had told her mother whilst she was helping her in the kitchen. Her mother had taken it well and had promised to help her all she could. Her father, a man of nearly 60, had had a heart attack when told and for a time his life was in the balance. Nevertheless, they stood by her and rejoiced in her baby, supporting her through difficult weeks when the tiny baby girl had to undergo a series of operations for a slight heart defect. Caroline brought her baby with her when she received her examination certificates.

The next time I saw Caroline was when her daughter was starting at the local infants' school. She called in with her after school. She also had a 2-year-old daughter and was cohabiting with a very disturbed and delinquent young man who had been a pupil in the unit the year before. She was already expecting a third child by her new partner who had only just had his seventeenth birthday. She had a council flat and they were both on the dole. Her parents were still very supportive of her and regularly baby-sat and took the little girls to buy shoes and outdoor coats.

Another case concerned Tony, the younger of two brothers who had been adopted when his brother was 3 and he was a baby. It was thought that it was an adoption within the family. The parents had never spoken about the circumstances surrounding the adoption though they had told me that the boys were adopted. Although both boys had a lot of problems with school and with the police, the parents were not unduly worried as the father had, as he said, 'been a bit of a lad' in his young days too. I was very worried about Tony as, apart from taking drugs himself, I felt he was also supplying to other pupils. When I called the parents in they said that this was not possible; Tony hated drugs so much he would not even touch a cigarette. I knew that he was almost a chain smoker, but the parents stuck to their story. In the end we had to exclude Tony because of the effect he was having on the group, and the fact that his parents backed him up against all the evidence. They were shocked when he was arrested for theft and suffered severe withdrawal symptoms whilst in custody. He has now just finished his third custodial sentence after leaving us in 1984. I do not think his problems were to do with adoption. In his case I think he was well adjusted to his family who operated outside the normal constraints of society.

I was far more concerned about Jeremy. He was an angelic looking boy whom I found difficult to equate with the appalling report I had had from his school. His parents, who brought him, both looked weary and despondent, but Jeremy wore a huge smile and seemed happy to be on the threshold of coming to the unit. I asked the parents how they felt about it and they shrugged helplessly. They said they really did not mind where he went as long as he was in school and doing something. They could not blame the other school for expelling him and they felt that they really had done all they could. They thought that Jeremy was bright but was wasting his time.

Jeremy was really more than we could handle at times. He was not afraid of doing or saying anything. He disrupted nearly every lesson unless it comprised oral questions and answers. This exception was because he had almost perfect recall and if you asked him what you had said a couple of minutes before he could repeat your words verbatim, even though at the time he was contorting himself and making everyone else laugh, or chattering to the others and distracting them. He seemed to be able to remember every French word he had heard (the family had often camped in France) and he could converse with me in French.

When he had to write he was very reluctant as his writing was a laboured scrawl which he could not get on to the line. He was incapable of setting out maths legibly, but in the City and Guilds examination (multiple choice) he gained a Distinction without staying in the exam for even half the time. Unfortunately, six weeks before his leaving date he disappeared from home and stopped coming to the unit.

During the time he was with us I had spoken to his mother at length and attended meetings with both parents. They had three older children who were born to them. All had done very well at school, two were at university and one was in the upper sixth. When he had joined the family, Jeremy had been nearly two and had, apparently, been spoiled by everybody. He had had a brother a few years older who had been fostered by another family for a number of years. Although they could not take both boys they agreed to let the older boy see his brother regularly. When the older boy's fostering broke down the family had him for holidays. Jeremy's disaffection with school coincided with his blood brother leaving school and becoming involved with criminal activity. The parents tried to stop Jeremy from going into the brother's territory, preferring the boys to meet at their home, but with the growing independence of adolescence this was more difficult to control. Jeremy's worst behaviour coincided with the older brother coming of age and demanding to know the facts about their parents. Apparently he had enjoyed telling Jeremy that their parents were criminally insane and in a mental institution. I do not know if this was a fact, but I think Jeremy's adopted parents and I understood why he was unable to concentrate on school work. Unfortunately he is still listed as a missing person and there is a warrant out for his arrest on a number of charges. He is not yet 17.

I am surprised that we do not have more adopted children as they have to cope with such a disrupted life history. Perhaps it is because of the commitment of adopted parents to what they have chosen to do.

Disrupting, disaffected, but still in mainstream education

There are many children who become chronically disruptive and disaffected in their mainstream schools, but do not fit into any of these categories. No teacher can be expected to make allowances for all these children reacting to their life histories. But perhaps it makes it a little easier to survive in the classroom if one is able to realise that some of the anger and hostility received is directed to the teacher because he or she seems more able to take it than the parent.

It must also be acknowledged that much disruptive behaviour can be directly traced to the inefficient or incompetent classroom management of a particular teacher or teachers. This might be the result of an unfortunate misjudgement when the teacher was appointed, of an unsuitable redeployment (pre-LMS), of lack of professional support, or personal ill-health. Even if this unfortunate misplaced person is not aware of his or her difficulties, colleagues will be. The pupils who bring a pattern of potential disruptive behaviour into school with them because of the factors I have mentioned may well be the ring-leaders in these classes. These pupils are also likely to cause concern to competent, well-organised teachers. These children, and those who have similar problems can best be coped with in a school that has a whole-school approach to discipline, with well planned meetings of staff at all levels, and a high standard of communication between staff and pupils.

I am only too aware that the children we have in the unit each year are the tip of a much larger iceberg. Mainstream teachers are dealing every day with pupils who are masters at stealing teaching time from the rest of the class, diverting their neighbours and eroding the teachers' confidence and well-being. I see mainstream education as being the ideal for the pupil, but I think that there is a point at which, if one child is putting a strain on the system in terms of time and the teachers' morale, he or she must be given specialist help even if it is not available in the school.

I think it is important that these pupils should not be allowed to unofficially drift away from school because it is easier to ignore their truancy than to have to cope with them in class. These are the children who often have the greatest need for adult attention, concern and support. These young people are part of a larger community. If, because a certain pupil is making a nuisance of him or herself in school his or her truancy is overlooked, it does not take long for others to see disruption in school as the way to obtain tacit agreement to leaving early. Some of the children who take this path to determine the end of their own school days might be the ones who most need help in the transition from school to work.

While looking at the child now presenting the problems it is important to try to find ways of helping the parents to make sure that their younger children do not repeat this pattern of disruption and disaffection because of perceived rewards or expectations. As I stated at the beginning of the chapter, many disaffected youngsters are the product of parents who felt their own education to have been an unproductive process. By using appropriate and sensitive means of relating with the troubled or troublesome pupil it might be possible to break this pattern so that they can support their own children's education positively. You can also help pupils to regain confidence in themselves and help them over the crucial stage of leaving school and finding a job.

There is one common factor in nearly all our pupils and many of their parents. They have a lack of commitment, not only to work, to punctuality, to attendance, to others outside the family but also to themselves. An example of this is when we organise an outing. First we discuss where everyone would like to go. Eventually we narrow it down to two or three choices. After further discussion we vote on which we shall arrange. Arrangements are made, letters are sent home and classroom preparation is done. The week of the trip arrives but still no consent forms have been returned. I quickly photocopy some more. Two or three are returned; as it is now the eve of the outing I tell those who swear they are coming but have forgotten their form, that they may give it to me on the station. It is arranged to meet on the station at 9.30 am. Out of 32 pupils, we have been led to expect 12 or 15 to turn up. It is more than possible that only four or five will turn up if it is raining. Often not one person who voted for the chosen venue has had the commitment to take part in the trip.

The idea of being committed to people and organisations outside the home and family is one which we are tackling in the curriculum. It is to be hoped that some of the 'windows' opened by recent education reform – parents as governors, opportunities for parents to see the school at work, links with local work-places, link courses at colleges, voluntary work in the community, frequent reporting between school and home, and child and tutor working together to produce a positive record of the pupil's achievements at school and elsewhere – will make schools more welcoming to all parents.

CHAPTER 4

Obsessions, Addictions and the Wrong Side of the Law

There is one concern that has constantly increased during my time with troubled and troublesome adolescents. It is a matter which causes in me a feeling of despair, frustration and helplessness. It is the almost indefinable consciousness that so many of our pupils are involved with drugs. There are so many problems about the extent to which teachers of secondary pupils can do anything about the 'drug problem' among young people of school age, yet it is an issue we cannot ignore.

I am angry when I hear of a 'drug problem in our schools'. I feel the responsibility for the problem should be placed where it belongs, not in our schools but in society. The only reason that it is any cause of concern in schools is because so many young people have been coaxed in to this shadowy world, at an age when they are still obliged to attend school. I am aware that there are a great many users of cannabis among all young people, and that there has been for some time. Some pupils come from families where cannabis is smoked openly indoors. Some teachers may have experimented with it whilst at college. This can trivialise our conception of the effect that its use can have on the pupils we are trying to teach.

Why worry . . . it's only cannabis?

I think it is important to remember that the habit costs at least £5 a day – quite a large sum of money for a young person, dependent for pocket money on the goodwill of parents or on the wage from a part-time job. Once a young person has put himself into the position where he is under pressure, or even expectation to buy, the likelihood worsens of his handling goods dishonestly, stealing, mugging and pick-pocketing. When he buys drugs and when he uses them he breaks the law, and by this act is known by others to be someone who is not afraid to act criminally. Therefore the dealer and his acquaintances 'have something on him'. As soon as he starts buying supplies he is part of a group of people who are seen to have little respect for the law.

To what extent can we be not only aware but known to be aware of law-breaking among our pupils? What is our responsibility to their parents and to society on this subject? If I know that a pupil is a user I explain to him that I have to inform his parent(s). I am aware that the greater the expression of shock and horror, the more likely it is that the parent(s) already know and it might even be a family habit, or at least condoned indoors. Sometimes the child totally denies the accusation and the parent accuses me of being a troublemaker, or challenges me to prove it. On just a few occasions, however, parents have expressed relief that I have confirmed their suspicions because now they feel they can begin to act confidently to try to control their child. Others look at me wearily and say, 'But they all do it, don't they?'. At this point I usually mention the cost, and they look uncomfortable and say they will look into what is happening.

It is a far bigger problem when I know that the pupil is actually supplying cannabis to others. I discovered 80 per cent of my intake one year was involved in the practice. None of them considered themselves to be dealers, however. I called one mother in to discuss it with me. Her son, Adrian, was already in quite a bit of trouble with the police and was due to appear in court on a number of charges. She seemed to be making a real effort to sort him out and support him at the same time. She attempted to reassure me about the cannabis resin that I had heard was changing hands, but focused on the question of profit-making rather than addiction. Apparently the boy's father, who lived in another borough, had access to a cheap supply and Adrian just brought back enough for himself and a few of his mates and their friends each week end. Any profit he made barely covered the cost of what he kept for himself! So you see he wasn't a dealer, was he?

For a long time I was too naïve to realise that dealing was going on under my nose. I saw no significance in the fact that during the last period of the morning or the afternoon pupils were extra edgy and excited. I showed only perfunctory interest in the groups of youngsters who hung about outside the unit for the pupils to emerge, and the cars, mainly BMWs and top-of-the-range Escorts, that would be there to meet pupils. They all knew that I recognised the smell, and they never actually used cannabis near the unit. I finally realised what was going on when one very unpopular boy was absent for a few days and I was besieged by youngsters from outside the school demanding to know where he was, asking for his address and phone number.

It then became clear that the men in the cars were the next link-up in the selling chain, and the other kids around the school were the customers. I later heard a boy from a very impoverished home telling another that he owed his dealer £380 because he had 'smoked more than he had sold' that week. The other boy was quick to offer to put him in touch with a different dealer who could supply him with a stronger type of resin on which there was a bigger profit margin. It was not surprising that this group of boys found it difficult to concentrate on any lessons except when I taught them 'relevant' material about percentages and fractions.

This was a vivid example of the part that motivation has to play in learning. Most drugs are sold in eighths and sixteenths. When our pupils become involved they often hesitate to tell the dealer that they do not understand these fractions. Therefore they can end up losing money instead of making it. I have never had such an attentive class as when I was teaching fractions to this group. One boy had been given bags containing an eighth, and was under the impression that two of these made a sixteenth. This boy checked and rechecked that he had understood properly. At the age of 15 several pupils were excited and amazed by the revelation that the smaller the fraction the larger the denominator was, a lesson they will not forget in a hurry, because of its practical application!

After this I involved the local drug squad in such an obvious way that the actual trade on my doorstep stopped – I think. I believe many teachers will be familiar with my dilemma. I did not want to put myself in the position of pupils being arrested on my premises for what was essentially an outside problem. On the other hand I could not ignore the fact that the law was being flouted under my nose.

When I had time to reflect on what was happening I became very concerned about the large sums of money that my pupils were involved in handling. I also realised that somewhere in the chain in which they had become links must be some much bigger criminals than they were, with much more at stake. I became even more alarmed at how easily I, as a bystander, could have become far more involved, had I not managed to stop the trade on my patch.

What does this have to do with teaching adolescents?

As well as their life histories, this obsession with drugs is another factor that distracts some of the unit pupils from their school work. I feel that my pupils are the tip of a much larger iceberg of pupils sitting in regular classrooms, unable to benefit from even the most thoughtfully adapted curriculum because of their preoccupation with legal and, increasingly, illegal drugs. When I have asked pupils why they have been excluded from school they often admit to having done anything to cause themselves to be sent out of class, 'because I was dying for a fag'. Many of them have been in repeated trouble because of their early tobacco habit.

It is possible that many readers, even now, will be recalling how sweet those moments were in the bike shed before school, and during break, as we shared a filter tip, and passed the mints before the bell went. There is a difference between this rebellion of the teens, and the teenager who is obsessed, or perhaps I should say addicted, with the need for any drug. The differences between cigarettes that are sold at the corner shop, and cannabis which is bought on the street corner are small, but significant. Indulgence in the latter is a criminal activity as the law stands in this country. Anyone dealing in the substance is a criminal in the eyes of the law. There is also the fact that the use of the latter is primarily to cause temporary changes in feelings and thus personality. The user is no longer in full control. This can have safety implications if it is used in public. It also questions how concerned we should be about the young person who is prepared to spend more money than he or she has in order to gain a few minutes escape from reality.

Nevertheless, I think we have to regard cigarette smoking among our school children with similar concern, in cases where it has become a real habit as opposed to an occasional, experimental act of rebellion. It is very much part of the confusion of adolescence – those who feel most inadequate in the classroom most wish to seem older and tougher than they are. Although there are other factors, it is interesting that every year a few adolescents in the unit give up smoking, a habit that they have had since they were 9 in some cases. Relinquishing their dependence on cigarettes is seen as a very adult thing to do and is usually the sequel to some tangible success. This year three pupils gave up soon after learning that they had gained a Level I Certificate in an external examination on numeracy. This coincided with a health education project on the dangers of smoking, but I feel that the success in the examination was more instrumental than the fears of serious illness in giving the pupils the strength to discard this prop. I am convinced that those pupils who have smoked tobacco from an early age are more likely to procede to other drug use than those who have not developed this habit, especially if they feel that they lead unsuccessful lives and that this is unlikely to change.

I therefore think there is a very strong case for sparing no efforts in educating against the use of tobacco by children. I am pleased that, at last, the Health Education Council seems to have abandoned its policy of illustrating how smoking ruins your health by showing films of middle-aged people practically on their death beds, since this is a spectre hardly likely to deter an 11-year-old. The Council's latest film, featuring Gary Lineker, shows what a 'walley' you look when you stride into a shop to buy ten cigarettes. All our pupils were scornful of how stupid young kids looked with cigarettes. The new film also has a cynical scene of tobacco magnates conferring to see how they can hook youngsters by selling single cigarettes. After seeing this film several of our pupils said that they wished they had seen it before they were hooked. They were also very impressed by a film by an Australian doctor. They identified very positively with the doctors who broke the law to deface cigarette advertisements and they were appalled at how advertising blatantly cons the public. It was this, rather than concern for their health, which prompted nearly all my pupils to express a wish to give up.

Can we influence children at all in their use of drugs? Naturally, in common with most schools, we also have a programme of education against drugs. It is unfortunate that much of the material designed to put teenagers off taking drugs offers them the risks and excitement for which so many of our pupils are eager. The story of the sudden and much publicised death of a teenager, followed by the graveside self-recriminations of inconsolable parents, is more likely to attract the teenager, who is using drugs as an escape from the realities of an unsatisfactory home life. By far the most impressive session of drug education for our group was when two of our local juvenile bureau policemen came in to give a talk. They arrived prepared to show a film but the projector didn't work. They proceded to confide in me some of the problems with drugs in the area. Because the pupils were given the impression that this was confidential information, they listened intently. They heard about the man who made a fortune passing off dried dog excrement as 'black Leb' (an expensive form of cannabis resin). They paled at the perfidy of the man who cut the heroin with cement when he couldn't obtain his usual scouring powder. No, they went on to confide, they could not tell them how many died because their blood solidified in the arteries, as they were still finding the bodies. The kids are surprised and scandalised to hear how many times heroin is cut and diluted with other substances before it reaches the customer. The thought of being conned is obviously more of a deterrent than the thought of being killed.

Since all pupils coming to the unit are over 14 years old, and most of them admit, in front of their parents, to smoking, I allow smoking outside during the official breaks. Were I to veto smoking completely I would probably spend the day waiting for smokers to emerge from the two lavatories. It would also become an effective way of diverting attention away from other problems and from school work. Smoking is always discussed at the initial interview and, if parents specifically ask me to make sure that their son or daughter does not smoke, I respect this, as long as they say it in front of the child.

'Drugs in the classroom'

We do have limited success at fighting smoking, which I feel is caused mainly by it no longer being an act of rebellion but an activity in the pursuit of which the pupils have to suffer fairly uncomfortable conditions, especially in bad weather. I think that recently the message from the health education films has been more appropriate for this age group, and has made some of them feel that they are now too old and too wise to smoke! However, I still feel totally frustrated with many pupils' obsession with smoking and drugs even in curriculum activities. If any opportunity to draw presents itself there is always the execution of re-occurring symbols and figures. Pupils in different years, and originating from different schools and different estates, will produce the same stereotyped drawings. A very common one is an Afro-Caribbean young man with a 'spliff' (a long tube in which tobacco and either cannabis resin or marijuana herb is mixed together and smoked) dangling from his mouth. Sometimes pupils will pencil a 'spliff' onto the lips of a picture in the same way that generations of school boys have added moustaches and spectacles to portraits. Almost invariably, when our pupils doodle on paper, it is to produce images such as these. There will sometimes be the 'spliff' in the process of being rolled, and then again with smoke coming out of it. There will also be stylised pictures of cannabis leaves or twin palm trees against a setting sun.

A few years ago I was mystified when pupils often added a beauti-fully drawn tomato or strawberry to a finished picture. I was in the foyer of a secondary school eight miles away, looking at the display of

CSE art, and saw the tomato and strawberry featured in several of the paintings. There was also a picture of a boy squatting by a river bank, watching a toy yacht sailing on a pond. There was smoke rising above his head. On closer inspection, the hull of the yacht was a partly rolled 'spliff'. It was identical to two pictures that had been drawn in the unit in the last few weeks, except for the number on the boy's shirt. They could not be the work of the same pupils as this school was in a different authority. I later learned from a youth worker that the number denotes the type of cannabis available.

The next time I saw the tomato being drawn I observed to the girl who was drawing it, 'Tomatoes are acid aren't they?'. She asked me how I knew. I then observed that strawberries were sweeter than tomatoes but not much. I thought perhaps they were symbols for two different supplies of LSD but a little later in the term I noticed that on some occasions the strawberry was either marked with an E or close to one so I hazarded a guess that it symbolised the designer drug, Ecstasy, and my suspicion was confirmed.

I am not sure whether adolescents do these drawings to indicate to each other the existence of supplies, or if it is part of their obsession with this scene and their eagerness to identify with it. One thing I am certain of is that it is a way of informing a new member of the group what is going on, and sounding them out on their knowledge. I would imagine that it would be quite difficult for a new pupil to be accepted in this group and not at least pay lip service to being interested in drugs. I think it is important for teachers in mainstream schools to be aware of this symbolism and be alert to any pressure being exerted by one group of pupils on others because of what might have been innocently drawn, or copied in the classroom by younger pupils.

A few years ago, a rather naïve young teacher spent two terms in the unit. Since he was an artist, he asked my permission to cover two rather shabby walls with murals. Imagine my horror when I returned from a meeting to find beautifully executed drug symbols covering the walls. The pupils were delighted with their work and all wanted to take photographs before I ordered it to be removed within the week.

In connection with this, I am always surprised at the number of caring, concerned parents who are seemingly happy for their teenage off-spring to wander round French and Spanish holiday resorts wearing T-Shirts sporting the universal symbol for cannabis, the five segment leaf, and the multi-purpose symbol for Ecstasy and LSD, a smiling face, like the ones I used to draw on the exercise books of good children, years ago! There is quite a strong likelihood of a young teenager who is sporting these symbols being offered the substances. It is not easy for a youngster, who is put in this position, to ignore the pressure.

I have asked my young cousin, Emma, who is an art student in a northern town, to draw some of these symbols for me. She has, without prompting, drawn those familiar to me in the south-east.

Obsession or addiction?

I feel it is the obsession with the drug phenomenon and its illegality that causes the problems with most of our pupils rather than their addiction to the substance as such. Although if life becomes too uncomfortable they will deny all involvement, they almost make sure that we know they have this side to their lives. Even in the more understanding environment of the unit they seem to need the excitement of risking our disapproval and anger. I think it is also a challenge to us to see if we will involve the police. Needless to say, involvement with drugs does provide a certain personal prestige among other pupils. There is no doubt that this obsession is of concern to us in the classroom. Although it does not indicate addiction, it certainly is a clear indication of usage. We have had afternoons when our pupils were docile and easy to talk to – though not to teach – because we realised that most of them were so high as a result of lunch-time indulgence that they did not have the energy or inclination to be their usual disruptive selves. It is at this stage we brace ourselves for the irritability and frustration of the 'let down' period, when the effect of the drug is wearing off.

'Unsteadily to school'

I believe that teachers in schools now often have to face a first class of the afternoon where some of the members are still inebriated with either drugs or drink. Although there has always been a certain amount of under-age drinking at weekends there is no doubt that pupils are now coming into school still 'hung over' from the night before. I am concerned about the number of my pupils who boast of weekends passed in a drunken stupour. I am shocked at the frequency with which some of them are picked up from the street in a totally insensible state and delivered home by the police. One can only speculate on the effects that the favourite 'special brew' can have on immature livers.

What should we as teachers do about this? Talking to the pupil about his or her condition can provoke a confrontation which will prevent the rest of the class receiving a full lesson. Ignoring the fact is far easier, but is this a neglect of one's duties *in loco parentis*? It is far simpler for those of us who teach adolescents in small units as we can stay with the problem and pick our moment during the day.

I feel that any pupil believed to be 'under the influence' at school should be carefully monitored, and should know that members of staff are aware of his or her condition. Any accusation of drinking or drug taking will be met with vehement denial by the pupil, but it is still important that it is not ignored. Although the young person will never admit to his or her problem he or she might try to keep it away from school. This is not a recipe for sweeping problems under the carpet. If the pupil is still at the stage where he or she is involved in school and wishes to do well, he or she might at least cut down his or her drinking or drug habit enough for it not to be evident at school. On the other hand if, instead, he or she avoids staff who intervene, or even avoids school altogether, then the problem must be picked up with his or her parents or carers.

It is important that all staff share factual knowledge about these pupils. Wherever the school is aware that there are a number of pupils who are regularly drinking there should be an attempt to formulate a whole-school policy. This can only be done if all incidents are noted and all difficulties which could be caused by alcohol abuse noted. It is important that any policy neither rewards nor humiliates the child but is consistent throughout the school. It is important that the child is not forced into a situation where he or she gains reinforcing attention and admiration from peers because of disrupting the class.

A very special need of adolescents is the opportunity to talk over problems regularly. With the changing of financial arrangements in schools, the senior management team, one of whom was often the 'pastoral head', is now more usually involved in activities to do with making the school more marketable. Any notion that there is a drug problem is going to be particularly threatening to this team of people, concerned with the school's popularity in the 'market-place'. I see a need for the coordinator of Special Educational Needs providing an ear for the concerns of pupils and other staff about such problems as suspected drug use as well as expertise with learning and behavioural difficulties.

What about health education

Adolescents in their final two years of statutory education need a different kind of health education from younger children. Although the resources for health education have improved greatly in recent years, and much of the material labelled for the use of 14- and 15-year olds is more suitable for a younger age group, where there is still a chance of prevention. We have to recognise that, especially for troubled adolescents, the years from 14 to 17 are often a time of reckless risk-taking and, in many cases, disturbing suicidal attempts. By dwelling on the dangers of drugs and drink we are often merely glamourising them. The approach, mentioned earlier, of emphasising the commercial benefits of getting young people hooked on expensive substances is often a much more effective one. Pupils become extremely indignant when they realise how much tax they are paying to the government when they buy cigarettes and drink.

Dealing with the problems

There are some young people who, at the age of 15, are already too addicted to smoking and drinking to give up that easily. One afternoon recently, one of my brightest girls, Julie, came into the unit barely able to walk straight. Her speech was slurred and her eyes were closing. Although I had confronted her several times about smelling of drink when she arrived in the afternoon, I had never before seen her in this state. I had sensed, during the previous few days that, despite her loud laughter and rumbustious acting-out behaviour, she was becoming more and more depressed. I knew that she had had difficulty in deciding with which parent to live, whether she should settle for a comfortable home with firm control, or a frugal one, lacking in physical comfort but with almost total freedom. I knew that she had settled for the latter. I had expressed my concern to her about this choice and had tried to encourage her to talk about the problems which I was sure still prevented her from being able to settle down to work. My comments had caused her to be extremely abusive to me and to accuse me of fabricating stories about her drunkeness. Yet I feared that she was in danger of being involved in an accident, or of being sexually abused, if she was frequently in this condition, without any responsible adult in control. I knew that she had twice been picked up drunk by the police in the last three weeks. I also felt there was a very strong possibility of alcohol poisoning as most of her intake each day was in the form of alcoholic beverages. Before I went home I referred the case to the local Social Services, and followed up my 'phone call with a letter, copies of which I sent to both her parents, to the Educational Welfare Officer and the school psychologist. By the time a child protection meeting was called the following week, she had already been admitted to hospital after overdosing.

There are still many problems in this case. Gradually I am regaining Julie's trust enough for her to start to take an interest in her school work. It will be an up-hill task and, although Julie is perhaps one of the most able girls it has ever been my pleasure to teach, I do not know if she will be stable enough to pass the examination she should be able to do quite easily. It is important that we should stay with her and give positive reinforcement to any attempt she makes to do the things that are appropriate to her age at this time. We shall remain aware of her problems but not in a way that she feels that this is the reason we are interested in her. It is important for a child like this that we are ready to give positive cognitive intervention in curriculum activities when she is conforming and doing her work. She would be the first to feel patronised by the well-meaning and ubiquitous, 'Oh, well done!', often given when a reluctant pupil turns in a mediocre piece of work. The more constructive response is to demonstrate an interest in the work produced. Thus, being engaged in conversation and having another source of information suggested to help enrich what she is writing, or being shown how to check back on a maths answer involves and dignifies the pupil who is trying to re-engage with work, when previously other problems have predominated.

It is important, especially in a unit or special class situation, not to let problems become a way of avoiding doing the school work. The way forward for these adolescents is through success in the curriculum. I am very suspicious when I hear of places where a young person could go with their problem any time of the day. It could totally disrupt the group if a member of staff were to withdraw at the beginning of the day to counsel an individual. I have found that when I make an arrangement to discuss a problem with a pupil at a specific time, he or she is ready and eager to talk then and much more is achieved.

After a visit to another unit, I was waylaid outside by some boys who asked if they could walk me to the station. During the 20-minute walk they passed the time by telling me all the dodges they had for avoiding work. The main one was to go in and say they had a problem. I was told that sorting this out could take 'all maths and quite a bit of

English'. I asked the boys whether they thought it fair that valuable time which could be spent preparing for examinations should be used for counselling when there were plenty of breaks when it could be done. One of them replied that he supposed they would not have so many problems if that happened. There is no doubt that many pupils do have genuine problems which they wish to discuss with a caring adult. My experience suggests that those pupils will be pleased to be allotted the opportunity to do this at a mutually convenient time outside lessons.

Television and video: a blessing or a curse?

As well as the problems caused by obsessions with prohibited substances and addictions to these same substances in some cases, the widespread ownership of video recorders has caused another set of problems. Many pupils come in to school, not hung over with drink and drugs, but tired from watching videos for many hours on end. I also noticed a dramatic increase in fatigue among my pupils from the time that ITV started screening films all night. Many of our pupils have TVs in their own rooms, and in areas where lorries frequently shed their loads, many pupils also possess their own video recorder. In many homes the film watched last thing at night, or in the early hours of the morning, has replaced the age-old pleasure of reading a chapter of a book, in bed, before switching off the light. Whereas the latter left something for the imagination to work on, the last video at night can leave the viewer with explicit and horrific scenes that form a lasting impression and disturb the sleep.

A separate issue from tiredness is the nature of the videos watched by many of our young people. From the film industry's earliest days there has been concern about the effect on young minds of the sex and violence portrayed. Many is the time I have gone to bed and hoped I would not have nightmares as a result of the horror film I have willed myself to watch with my now adult sons. This has been watched in company, with the light on, and with protective comments, like 'you can see where the latex meets the flesh' and 'you can see that's just a model'. This is a very different situation from watching a film alone, in the darkness of the bedroom. Young people watching videos in these situations often run and rerun a short sequence of particularly brutal violence, and often have access to extremely violent adult sex videos, which portray as everyday occurrences sexual practices which demean and brutalise girls and women. One boy of 15 in my unit was always exhausted on a Wednesday morning. It transpired that his father entertained several of his mates for an evening of porn while his wife was at bingo. He was quite happy for his son to join them. However, since it was Barry's job to get the videos back to the shop in the morning, he kept them in his room overnight and, when he was sure the rest of the family were asleep, looked at the 'best bits' over and over again. I was sickened when I overheard him relating some of the scenes to his friends in the playground. It was not surprising that he and his friends had what I can only describe as a sick attitude to girls and women. He even referred to his mother as 'the old dog', and rarely referred to the girls as anything but 'slags' and 'tarts'. Some of these attitudes were doubtless learned from his father, but I have no doubt at all that they were dangerously reinforced by his preoccupation with violent and perverted sex as seen on videos.

Adolescents and the law

It is not surprising that many of these adolescents who give us cause for concern because of their obsessions and addictions are already known to the courts. In fact involvement with the law is probably as consuming an obsession for some of them as drugs, drink and sex videos. When boys first arrive in the unit, they vie with each other to have the worst court case pending. I found out very early in my career with this group that, if I wanted to obtain a successful piece of work, I could do no better than to focus it on crime or criminals. When we were told that we had to do literature and creative writing with all pupils I was dismayed. Many of our pupils had long ago dismissed creative writing as 'useless...who needs it?'. They also dismissed reading anything except the racing papers and teenage comics as totally unnecessary.

used the poem *Nile Fishermen* by Rex Warner. When I told them to read it through and tell me where the police were, who they were going to arrest and why, there was immediate interest. They worked in pairs and read it over and over with each other until they had 'cracked' it. I was then able to talk to them about some of the imagery used. They agreed that the story would have taken several columns in *The Sun* and that poetry was a clever way of telling a story in a different way. Some of them wrote it up as a story for a newspaper. Others wrote a poem about a similar incident. During the next session they all wrote a very vivid account, again in poetry or prose, about an arrest they had witnessed – real or imaginary – and they did not have to tell me which.

By this time they were really identifying with the *Nile Fishermen*, and wrote touching and beautiful letters to their wife, Fatima, from the confines of their remand cell. I was heartened to read these tender letters of concern and explanation about why they had broken the law, and pleased that they had thought to remind her to collect the nets from the beach where they had been dropped, 'in case some other b---d comes and chores [steals] them'.

Since favourite reading for this group has been the biographies of Ronald Biggs and of the Kray twins, I have set assignments based on these books. I was pleased when one boy came to me and said, 'I thought that the Krays were great but, having to really think about what they did, and what happened, makes me depressed about crime. It's a bit of a waste of time, isn't it?'.

My most ambitious exploitation of this interest in crime has been the studying of Shakespeare's Julius Caesar with this group. They soon identified Cassius as a 'bad lot', they hated Casca for his smoothness, and called him 'the yuppie' (this is a serious insult from this group). They had a very heated debate over whether Cassius and Casca were 'queers', and they despised Brutus for being flattered, feeling that he should have realised that the letters through the window were 'a wind up'. I have made a series of differentiated work-cards on this play for students to work on alone or in pairs, and, much to my surprise, these have proved very popular and are often requested when other lessons finish early. By starting from an interest that is already there I have been able to achieve far better work from these pupils than they, or their parents, thought they could achieve.

Obsessions, addictions and the curriculum

Perhaps the pupils' interest in the law is the easiest topic to exploit in the curriculum. Their interest in drugs is exploited when we make our annual visit to the Tate Gallery and look closely at the pictures of Richard Dadd (The Fairy Fellow's Master Stroke is the favourite). I remind them that this was done in an asylum as Dadd was shut away from an early age. A look at drugs in the nineteenth century, and the talented lives they ruined is often surprising to this generation of adolescents who think that it was their parents, in the halcyon days of the 1960s, who discovered drugs.

Their interest in the law can also be exploited in religious education. I challenge them to find any contemporary law that is not part of the Ten Commandments. They find it difficult to realise that all our basic laws originate from the Bible and were written on tablets of stone. We then look at how the punishments have changed and discuss why society demands retribution for law breaking. They are interested to hear about Islamic Law and the connection between the laws of civilisations and Health and Safety regulations. They are interested in how the dietary laws of both Jews and Moslems were appropriate for peoples living in hot, sometimes insanitary conditions. They are dubious about the 'no alcohol' rule in the Koran and understand that it is concerned with the desirability for man always to be in control of himself. This provides a good topic for discussion.

Legal procedures and their effect on school children

Some unit pupils find it quite chastening when I point out that their addictions and obsessions often involve a loss of the freedom to which they should be entitled. Many, when they are referred to the unit, are awaiting a court case. Despite the outward bravado, I feel that the pressures caused by the drawn out processes of the law can cause an adolescent, who is just about managing at school, to finally become too disaffected to cope. Young people are often called into court four or five times, only to be sent away for 28 days because reports are not available or a vital witness is missing. These delays put tremendous strain on some families and, if a solicitor and a barrister are involved, the youngster tends to have to be absent for appointments on a number of occasions. For reasons of their own, most barristers seem to try to convince the youngster that, short of a miracle, he will be locked up. Although, if they looked around, they would realise this is very unlikely, especially for a first offence, it often means that the boys and girls concerned do not feel it is worth doing any work until the case is over.

Another result of delay is that the youngsters' misdemeanours receive attention out of all proportion to their importance. This can result in the miscreants becoming heroes among their peers. Almost invariably pupils exaggerate to me the magnitude of the trouble in which they are involved. By the time the case comes to court the parents often feel that the young person has already suffered enough. Any bad behaviour before court is excused because of the strain that the youngster is feeling, and one feels that a year of education is often totally wasted because of the way juvenile crime is handled.

There were two boys who were known to have burnt down a local building. They had admitted it but, on the spur of the moment, decided to say another boy was also there. This boy had a cast iron alibi, but time had to be spent checking out the boy's story. Finally a date for the hearing was set, almost a year after the deed. One of the boys then changes his plea to not guilty on the morning and a different solicitor had to be found since he was now giving evidence against the other boy. For some reason it was decided that the other boy should also have a different solicitor. He had meanwhile changed his plea to not guilty on two of the three charges; another two months passed with no hearing being possible. The case was heard three months later but it was decided that it had to go to the High Court. On the second day in the High Court, almost two years after the fire, the case was thrown out because of lack of police evidence on one of the charges.

Everyone knew the boys had done it. The boys returned to school triumphant. Their feeling of power was tangible. There was no way that we could ever effectively control them again, since they had defeated the acknowledged might of British Law. I know many teachers of adolescents who could tell similar tales. Just another way in which disruption comes from within and without.

What can the school do?

To what extent should schools be concerned with the criminal side of the pupils' lives? There is a greater accountability in schools than ever before and resources have to be used with care, especially human resources. However, schools cannot ignore the influence that some older pupils involved in drugs have on some of the more vulnerable younger pupils. There are also safety issues involved if pupils are present in the building under the influence of drink and drugs, and there is a fire risk if pupils gather to smoke or inhale flammable substances in hidden corners.

I think that senior management must be involved and be prepared to work with the police in any case where pupils are known to have drugs on the premises, or if it is suspected that trade is taking place at the school gates. It is important for pupils to know that law-breaking cannot be condoned on school premises, and those who are profiting from the sale of prohibited substances must be dealt with by the community, not the school.

It is also important for those pupils who are using drugs but want to stop, to know that they have support within the school. Since schools cannot afford to have school counsellors, perhaps work with this group should be part of the special needs provision of the school and budgeted accordingly. I believe every secondary school should have a member of staff who is able to work sensitively with pupils on these issues. I do not think we, as teachers, can make much difference to what is happening with drugs in the community at large, but it is important that schools prevent both the use and the trade in drugs on their premises.

CHAPTER 5

Troublesome Adolescents – Troubled Teachers

Many teachers suffer worry and frustration because of the behaviour and attitude of a growing group of adolescents. In Chapter 3 I described some of the life histories and family traditions which may cause many of these problems encountered in the classroom.

However much we understand and sympathise with our pupils, we are teachers with a teaching job to do. A very difficult and stressful part of this job is trying to engage reluctant pupils whilst, at the same time, catering for the needs of the rest of the class. Some of these other pupils might be highly motivated and have very clear ideas about what they are hoping to gain from their education. It is important that all pupils are given the best situation possible to reach their full potential.

Why do they make it so difficult?

Most of us are familiar with the situation where we enter the classroom to present a new piece of work, knowing that two or three pupils will somehow try to sabotage the lesson. This may start with an exaggerated yawn, an anti-social noise or smell which reduces the rest of the class to mirth or disgust, or there may be a low murmur of unsuppressable conversation. There are some members of the class whose school career has been so devoid of any positive feeling of success or interest that the first reaction to being taught in any lesson is to exercise avoidance tactics. One of the main strategies may well be to try to prevent the teacher, for as long as possible, from engaging any of the class in the lesson. Another could be to ensure that when the teacher does engage the class it is only done by letting the disrupting group continue on their own terms, perhaps engaging in low conversation, doodling on paper and not actually becoming involved in the listening or writing part of the lesson.

It is important to realise that, although only two or three will risk the consequences of causing disruption, others give passive support such that without these supporters, the disrupter would be powerless. For some disrupting pupils, the approval and admiration of their peers is the most positive reinforcement they receive during their school day. This behaviour also carries a fairly high risk factor, another 'plus' for many underfunctioning adolescents. A young man I know very well explained to me once that the only thing that made him able to tolerate the boredom of being in lessons he did not understand, was the excitement of seeing how far he could go with 'winding up the teacher' before he was sent to the head. He felt the punishment he received on the few occasions he miscalculated was a small inconvenience for the excitement and alleviation of boredom thus gained. He admitted that there were some pupils who became fed up with his antics, but, while he still had supporters, he continued. As GCSE examinations approached and others began to want to make up lost time, he simply stayed away until it was time to leave school. He had lost all confidence in his ability to succeed with any learning. There was no attempt by the staff to re-engage him in school. At 16 he had nothing to show for 11 years at school, since he was never disruptive enough to be sent to a special unit. Along with many of his friends it was easier for the staff to let him drift away than battle with his disruption and disaffection.

I often compare my pupils' brains to computers into which that dreaded scourge, the computer virus, has penetrated. The virus has been created from the effect of their life histories and all the other emotional luggage they bring with them into the classroom. If we wish to bypass that learning-resistant virus, our input has to be planned with this in mind. Those whose learning is blocked by the 'virus' must be given the opportunity to 'dump' as much as possible of the unhappy and frustrated feelings they have about the last time they tackled this subject. Until this has been done the pupils will not be receptive to new learning. Sometimes just the introduction of the lesson can trigger these memories of failure, conflict, tedium and anger. The pupils might be reminded of events in their life histories such as the death or divorce of parents, sexual abuse, physical abuse, eviction, or other disruptive events to which many of our pupils' chaotic households are prone. To this day I connect the death of my father, when I was 6, with reading *The Radiant Way* book 4, and the intricacies of words with 'gh' in them. For years after I panicked if I thought a 'gh' might be necessary, often inserting it where it should not be and omitting it where it should be. If took me a long time to gain confidence in spelling. In the case of our pupils who often lack the opportunity and the articulation to talk about their difficult memories, these feelings of failure or incomplete mastery might release into the system a larger outbreak of the 'virus' than our input can bypass, and nothing will remain in the memory longer than it takes us to say it.

A few years ago I did a case study of Darren, a 15-year-old boy who appeared a bright, articulate young man. It was almost impossible to persuade him to attempt any written work in maths or English but in oral English, geography, French, science, history and RE he displayed a very good knowledge that indicated a well developed aural memory. I managed to obtain records of Darren's schooling, right back to the infants' school. It emerged that his parents' marriage had broken up during the weeks before he started school, and his mother had arranged to start work on the first day of term. By special arrangement she had left him in the school hall with the school keeper over an hour before school started and an hour before his teacher arrived. His teacher reported that he always appeared very tired during the morning and would often fall asleep after he came in from play and had to be woken up to eat his lunch. There was concern that he was weepy during the afternoon and was sometimes still waiting for his mother after the teacher had left, but there was no evidence of deliberate neglect. Indeed, there were very positive reports about how caring his mother was and the bond between her and her son. Yet, although Darren was always well cared for, by the end of the first year there were already concerns about his progress. The daily routine of waiting for school to begin and for his mother to collect him afterwards continued throughout the infant school, and on transfer to junior school Darren was described as a 'pale, quiet, permanently tired little boy who is finding it difficult to concentrate'. It is not difficult to understand that this seemingly endless school day had blunted this little boy's interest in learning.

After Darren transferred to junior school, his mother entrusted him to the care of a neighbour's child on his journeys to and from school. This gave him a shorter time in school but more time to 'run with the lads'. It was at this time that he started to get into trouble, including truanting. The only positive experience he seems to have had of school was when, at the age of 9, he was in a class where all the work was focused around a visit to London Zoo and to the Natural History Museum. There were examples of writing and drawing he had done at that time in his file. When I spoke to him about this project, almost seven years later, he could still remember certain exhibits at the museum with some clarity and he had retained an interest in the blue whale. His teacher at that time had obviously bypassed the 'virus' with his lively and imaginitive input and given this little boy his first feeling of success at school.

After a great deal of 'dumping' of old feelings of aggression against school, and even more aggressive feelings about his step-father of three years standing, we managed to persuade Darren to produce some work and he passed in the Level I City and Guilds Foundation Course examinations just before he left.

The behaviour I described at the beginning of this chapter will often tell us when there is this resistance to learning, although we might never know what has happened in the child's life to cause it. In order to involve everyone in the class on an equal footing from the beginning of the lesson, I acknowledge that everyone will have some experience of having done something about the topic before and I ask them to tell me when they did it and anything they remember about what the lesson was like. I do not ask if they can remember any facts about the subject, although this is frequently demonstrated, but I concentrate on when and where they did it. Before long I will learn a great deal about how they felt about the way they were taught at this time and how much they can remember. If this is done successfully, a number of pupils will be expressing quite strong feelings, and the lesson could be a noisier session than usual and will need careful 'chairing' to make sure every-one has a chance to have their say. The advantage is that the speaking is 'legal' and is not linked with achievement, but with experiences which all have.

Obviously an exercise like this is easier to achieve in a small unit or in a class where pupils are of similar ability. In a mixed-ability class where there are also high achievers it is important that no one is scorned because of what they say, although pupils will already be aware that some of their peers were more successful at learning than they were at a much earlier stage. Being able to discuss learning experiences in an open forum might well break down some of the resentment, often manifested in ridicule, against the 'boffs' in the class, as well as benefiting those who feel threatened by the possibility of having to display inferior skills. There is little doubt that in every class there are also some pupils who, while not acting out, are also underfunctioning because of other preoccupations. Although it would not be appropriate for them to express these problems in this forum, establishing an ethos of open discussion can help them to be able to share their feelings eventually.

At the end of this exercise, not only have unpleasant memories been dumped, and any learnt facts recalled, but the teacher also has a very clear idea of where he or she must start with each pupil.

Differentiation in the classroom

If the class is one where there is a wide range of ability there is potential for disruption and disaffection at both ends of the range, and there is little chance that a lesson aimed at the middle ability group will succeed unless the teacher has an extremely compelling personality.

Although some of the class might have poor reading skills, it is important that they are not given materials to use that are obviously designed for younger children. The pupils at the other end of the ability range will also need materials that fully engage them and do not leave them trying to find devices to fill in time. These children will usually have the motivation to extend an open-ended task if there are the resources available, and if they receive regular encouragement in the form of interest from the teacher. Also they will not feel so vulnerable to the ridicule of the class as the 'remedial' pupil who dreads the taunt that he is doing 'baby work'.

One of the most successful projects I have undertaken recently was the study of a Shakespeare play with a group of 15- and 16-year-olds whose attainment levels ranged from a potential 'B' grade in English GCSE to one pupil who had a reading age of only 7. It may seem that a Shakespeare play was an unwise choice in literature for such a disparate group. It was done, however, because they *all* wanted to do it, and they wanted to do it because they see studying a Shakespeare play as confirmation that they are grown up. When the pupils were presented with the opportunity to 'dump' all the feelings they had about previous lessons on Shakespeare, initially there had been many negative statements about incomprehensible language, old-fashioned stories and boring lessons. However, several pupils had a considerable number of positive recollections to share. Most had heard of the Rose and the Globe Theatres. Two very able girls had studied *Macbeth* and thoroughly enjoyed it; one of the poor readers spoke enthusiastically about his previous school's production of 'Julius Caesar', and was eager to recommend it to the others. Although when I had first introduced the idea there had been cries of 'boring' and 'crap', by the end of the 'dump' they were eager to start.

I started by reading aloud the first act, with pupils volunteering for parts. I was concerned when one of the least fluent readers wanted to read, but it was his choice and he accepted quiet prompts with grace. After a few scenes, when there was a natural break in the story, we discussed what had happened and then watched the play as far as we had read on a video. The following lesson I put out 10 work-cards with tasks on them. The tasks were such that pupils were able to tackle them at their own level of competence. Some opted to work together with one gathering information and the other writing it down. Some tasks involved finding a famous speech, copying it, taking turns in reading it to a partner to decide which words should be stressed, and discussing what it was about. In each case the poorer readers paired with a good reader and the good reader was pleased to read first. The poor reader, who was very dependent on the spoken word for meaning, was a good critic of expression, and after having heard the speech read a number of times was able to read it himself with adequate fluency. The more able pupil of the pair benefited from being in a 'teaching' role and, when they were discussing the meaning, there was little difference in ability as the type of language was new for each while many of the sentiments were familiar.

All the written assignments were open-ended enough for each pupil to decide on his own level of response. Although one boy wrote a short account of a conspiracy which had nothing to do with the one in the play, it was the first piece of sustained, coherent writing he had completed and was therefore as successful on that count as the work of the girl who was able to identify persuasive and flattering language and make an attempt at analysing the complementary roles of the characters. I think the value of this project has been proved by the number of dusty copies of Shakespeare plays that have been brought in for me to see, as well as a few *Lamb's Tales from Shakespeare*, which seems to have been a favourite Sunday School prize in the 1930s and 1940s. It is obvious that the group was proud of reading a real play and took their enthusiasm home with them.

When I am teaching a mixed group I find differentiated work-cards, which require the work to be done in one's own book, more successful than common work-sheets, even if they provide for work at different levels. The fact that only one pupil can use a particular card on any one day makes the comparisons much more difficult and it is not so obvious that the slower pupils have achieved less than others in volume of work. If there is a request for a certain card that is being used I can quickly make a similar one at a suitable level for the pupil who has asked for it. This merely adds another card to the collection and prevents any pupil from being hurried because of his card being needed by someone else.

Almost inevitably, when a new group arrives, most of them tell me that they are hopeless at maths. The girls in particular seem to lack all confidence, although initially they tend to display superior ability to the boys in this subject. As all the pupils gain confidence and progress is made by all, there is little difference in the final examination results of the two sexes. One of the first subjects I tackle with any new group is the dreaded fractions. In other units I have seen 15- and 16-year olds doing pages of addition, subtraction, multiplication and division when they first arrive, and it has often been suggested to me that we should start with the basics and build up. However, these young people have already had 10 years in schools. Their skills might be rusty from lack of use but they are there, and with the right stimuli, we will capitalise on them. I do have a box of basic number cards and occasionally a pupil requests the use of it in order to build up confidence, but I do not offer it generally as I feel it is reminiscent of an earlier stage of education. If I start with fractions, and do this subject carefully and thoroughly, all the basic rules will be revised and put into play when needed.

The first action after the usual 'memory dump' is to list related words and to work out a definition for fraction. In doing this it is established that the more pieces a whole is broken into, the smaller the pieces. The denominator is established as the *name* given to the pieces. If you nominate someone, you name them. The numerator is identified as the *number* of those pieces. If you want to know how numerous a group is you count it. Some of the group have heard these words, and been baffled by them. Although they do not need to use these terms I find that pupils are eager to use the proper vocabulary and making associations between words is an aid to memory. Before we go further there is an opportunity in quizzes and games to use the facts that have been learnt thus far.

With adolescents who have difficulty with learning because of other clutter in their minds, it is important to make sure that the main points of any lesson are internalised and made their own before moving on. In common with the computer, when our young people leave the building to go home, they switch off, and any memory that has not been consciously 'saved' might well be lost by the next session.

Methods have to be found to 'save' what they have learnt. Those that involve pupils talking together about the work seem to be the most effective aid to memory. This can involve a quiz, in two teams, where each person has to think up a question to ask the other team. The idea of individuals asking a question but the team answering means that everyone takes part but no one is put in the position of having to display ignorance. All the pupils realise that they must know the answer to the question they are asking, and it is a good idea to have two or three ready in case someone else asks theirs first. Another method is to ask groups of pupils to prepare a poster or simplified page of writing and illustration which would help younger children to understand the subject. Pupils tend to make sure they are in a group with someone who writes legibly and someone who can draw. Here it is important that the teacher moves from group to group to make sure pupils are on task.

In whatever teaching is done, it is important to use as many different ways as possible to reinforce each point, so as not to seem repetitive. I am very aware when I am teaching school leavers that this is their last chance and that I have to get it right. This means having work-cards, computer games and board games at every level of achievement. Experience has taught me that it is important to add new materials and reinforcing activities at nearly every session in order to keep all these pupils interested. In order to avoid using materials that are obviously designed for junior children, much of the equipment has to be home-made. However, there are some good quality plastic domino-type maths and spelling games on the market which are not obviously 'baby games'. I have found these very useful for pupils who are still making mistakes as a mistake made in a game can easily be corrected without leaving any permanent record. There are games to cover most mathematical concepts, and I consider time spent by two pupils discussing how to fit the dominoes together and checking on each other's final arrangement is as well spent for these reluctant learners as time spent writing sums out on paper, or filling in a work-sheet. Any game that can be devised that will involve four playing together competitively is extremely effective in internalising the concepts. In a mainstream classroom there would clearly need to be a number of games available.

In all the teaching I do with these troubled adolescents I feel that the actual cooperation and discussion between them during lesson times is the most important factor in building up their self-esteem. At first they find it very difficult to articulate their own feelings but, if it is obvious to them that what they are saying is being taken seriously and respected, their confidence grows and I am always pleased when I am challenged on an answer, a method or an opinion, as I then know that they are actually working it out for themselves.

In a large class it is far more difficult to have this level of interaction between pupils, so it is important, especially in a long lesson, or a lesson with less able children, that a period of legitimate conversation, in small groups, is planned. However, to prevent this becoming an exchange of gossip, the teacher must make the aim of the exercise clear and make sure that a spokesperson from each group has the opportunity to share their conclusion with the rest of the class. During this period it will be necessary for the teacher to move around the class and make sure everyone is on task, often bringing the pupils back on to the subject rather than reprimanding them for wasting time. If each group has a scribe whose task is to produce a list or result on a piece of paper it will be easier to check pupils are on task. The groups should be small enough to make sure all children are full engaged, but large enough to be able to support a child who is less confident. I would suggest at least three but not more than four. All children should know how long they have and should be told when the time is nearly up. If a teacher has not used this method before it is best to start with a short period and say at the outset what signal will be given to indicate that talking should cease.

With the kind of differentiated teaching I have described, records can become a nightmare unless kept up-to-date as the lesson progresses. All the learning in my unit is criteria-based as, from the time they are admitted, all our young people are preparing for the City and Guilds of London Foundation Course examinations. (Success in these examinations indicates that a student has the literacy and numeracy skills to be able to follow most of the City and Guilds courses leading to qualification in a trade). Every work-card is headed with the criteria it covers and each student has a record-sheet listing these requirements. At the end of each session the record-sheets are completed to show the objectives covered during the lesson. A pupil who has spent more time on written exercises than reading tasks will quickly notice the shortfall and know that next time it would be wise to start on a reading exercise. Because there is equal emphasis on oral skills in the English syllabus, it is important that we listen carefully when pupils are engaged in the kind of conversation exercise described above so that we can credit them for such objectives as 'identifying factually inadequate statements', 'using appropriate body language to emphasise a point', and 'using appropriate language for the situation and audience involved'. Pupils never fail to be pleased to see their oral record being completed with achievements.

This system gives all our pupils a clear expectation of success being within their grasp. It also presents them with a valid reason to demand the teacher's attention at regular intervals, to check on a task or mark the record. If they are unable to complete all the coursework assessment objectives to obtain a pass certificate, they will, in any case, qualify for a City and Guilds Profile which will show any employer what they have achieved.

'Don't patronise me!'

In different ways our pupils say this to us over and over again. They know if their work genuinely merits a compliment or if a compliment is given purely as an attempt to be friendly. They are immediately suspicious of any adult who comes in and tries to curry favour by using the type of language they use with each other. They see this as demeaning and an affront to their dignity.

When talking to pupils I use the same vocabulary that they hear me using with other adults. If I can see that they do not completely understand what I have said, I reiterate it in a slightly different way. Because there is an atmosphere where no one is ridiculed, pupils will often ask me the meanings of words I use and, within the next hour will be using them themselves. This vocabulary-building in their last year at school will give them confidence in communication in the wider society of the work place. At all times I talk to them as adults, who are interested in adult issues. Anything less would be an insult to these young adults. They become extremely irritated and feel patronised when well-meaning visitors talk to them, using swear words and commenting on what they believe to be the music of the day. I learned very early on not to presume to know what music was popular, even though for much of the time I have been surrounded by my own teenagers' music. Presumably, knowing that adults hate your music is one of the pleasures of being a teenager, and any adult who expresses approval is seen either as a phoney or an intruder!

Can the curriculum control behaviour?

There is no doubt that the right kind of curriculum – that is, the one which holds the possibility of success for every pupil – can certainly reduce the disruptive behaviour in classrooms. This curriculum has to be in place from the very beginning of the child's education. Just as a curriculum that is irrelevant and beyond their grasp can alienate the majority of pupils and cause disaffection, if not disruption, a well planned curriculum can engage all but the most disturbed and damaged adolescents. For many years the school system has been geared to examinations which were designed by university boards as the first steps in a process for selecting those who would one day become graduates. The sifting-out process began at the end of the fifth year. The disparity of expectation between different groups of children became, paradoxically, more defined in many comprehensive schools than in the former selective system, especially where the local grammar and secondary modern schools had been amalgamated. It was not unusual for pupils to be divided into a GCE stream, a CSE stream or a non-examination stream soon after the first term at secondary school.

With the GCSE examination for all, there should now be no need to distinguish between groups of pupils from the first year. I welcome the GCSE as an examination that is criteria-based rather than norm-referenced. Any pupil who works steadily throughout their school career, and has no crisis to contend with during the last two years, should have as good a chance as any other of obtaining a fair grade in this examination. The fact that success is dependent on a certain percentage of course-work means that examination nerves, proneness to hay fever in the summer, and problems on the day of the written papers are not as disastrous as they were with GCE, where a bad day could negate all the work of the previous five years. When pupils progress through the attainment targets and levels of the National Curriculum, provided they are given suitable intervention as a result of regular assessment, each child should reach Key Stage 4 ready to commence work on the GCSE course. To this extent, success in the curriculum should reduce the level of behaviour problems. Only time will tell whether pupils will receive the help that their first tests at 7 may indicate they need. I wonder how Darren, the boy who spent such long hours in his infant school, would have performed in this first test, and what kind of help would have been offered. His teachers were perfectly aware that his progress was being blocked by tiredness and apathy rather than by learning difficulties, but perhaps only support given to his mother would have solved this situation.

If we look through the records of our pupils, many of them were causing concern at the end of what would now be Key Stage 1. Some had already been through the break-up of their parents' marriage, a reconstruction of their family, the death of a parent or a crisis caused by eviction, imprisonment or illness. That many of them achieved as much learning as they did at this stage is a great tribute to themselves and their teachers. For many of these adolescents, the primary school was a much-needed safe haven from their very stormy home life. When I ask them to write or talk about their school life they almost always describe their primary school with great affection. It is interesting how often, in a period of 12 years, the names of the same good and caring teachers have been mentioned time and time again.

It remains to be seen whether the demands of Key Stage 4 will help pupils of the kind I have been describing. In the unit we have operated a completely alternative fifth year curriculum, which could not be matched in any way with the one that pupils have left. Although critics would say that this deprives our pupils of access to the range of activities provided in mainstream education, its advantage is that it is one which has involved and interested most of our troubled and troublesome adolescents. Because this group is reluctant, initially, to do anything that they do not feel has a direct application to their life after school, maths and English are concerned largely with filling in forms, understanding pay-slips, budgeting, reading safety regulations, calculating the cost of do-it-yourself jobs, writing letters and using the telephone effectively. I think it is an important recognition of the realities of adult life that a number of our English course-work assignments involve leaving a clear message on an answerphone.

At the time of German unification in 1989 there were advertisements in our local job-centre for labourers willing to join sub-contractors doing repairs and rebuilding dilapidated property in East Germany. This provided the stimulus for learning German. After five weeks most of my pupils were able to fill in a form in German, read illustrated safety regulations, and write a letter describing the accommodation they would like. They also wrote letters to a German friend of mine who is a painter and decorator, asking what qualifications they would need for painting and decorating. They were able to understand from the reply, written in German, that they would have been expected to complete a recognised trade course. They were clearly delighted at being able to correspond in a foreign language. German was a good choice as it has so many similar words to those in English and one boy suggested that it was more like cracking a code than learning a language. Our pupils, with their small amount of practical German, had gained the confidence to try to learn a language. I am sure that the small amount they did would enable them to take advantage of a more comprehensive course later. It certainly helped to erase earlier failure in French from their memories.

Of course our curriculum is not centred around the world of work alone, as the example of Shakespeare work earlier in this chapter illustrates. It would be a pity if, after 11 years of education, our pupils were unfamiliar with the work of any of the great authors, artists or composers. Because none of us is an art specialist we use books of reproductions of famous works of art to encourage attempts at drawing and painting. Often it is only when trying to copy a stretch of Canaletto water than a pupil realises the number of unexpected shapes and colours there are in a simple object. The pointillism of Seurat has been a favourite technique to copy, and some attractive and original work has been done. When we visited the National Gallery, there was great excitement when the pupils spotted paintings that we had discussed in school. It was also important for them to be seen by others to be 'in the know'. One boy was reprimanded for touching the painting. We were, however, sympathetic to his desire to feel the texture that he was delighted to recognise from the book he had read.

Whilst everyone is busy doing art, there is the taped music of a famous composer playing. The name and a few, usually racy, details of the composer's life are written on the board. At first there was resistance to listening to this type of music, but I pointed out that there might be times in their lives when they wished to object to certain kinds of music and that would be difficult to do if they did not know to what they were objecting. I was really pleased when one boy came in and commented that he did not like the Tchaikovsky that was playing. I asked him why. He said it was 'a bit heavy and jumbled for the early morning. Mozart or Chopin are better when you have got a hangover'. I offered to change the tape but he declined the offer as no one else had objected to it. This was a boy who had been totally opposed to any kind of classical music when he had first come. Several parents told us that their off-spring have asked them for some classical tapes and sometimes play them as background music.

Maps of areas which are in the news are put on the wall and regularly up-dated. Since in any 12 months there is usually trouble or natural disasters in every continent, this strategy effectively provides the motivation to study a wide range of geographical topics. There is no doubt that being able to inform their parents the background of certain news items gives our pupils status within their homes as well as the practice of serious communication.

Newspapers are an important resource for geography, English and maths. Most comprehensions are taken from newspapers – usually short, rather bizarre stories. Graphs and pie charts cut out of the money section of the papers provide relevant, up-to-date maths material. When I found out that colour supplements, not sold on a

Sunday, were dumped on a Monday, I arranged with my local newsagent to collect all his left-overs. This means that I frequently have a dozen or so of the same magazine — an excellent source of class reading material. All too often homework is accidently lost on the way home, or the book defaced by another member of the family at home. Since we discard the colour supplements within a few weeks they provide an excellent source of up-to-date material for homework and it does not matter if a sibling puts moustaches, or worse, on all the faces. Before this I felt able only to allow old books to go home and these were often too dated to be interesting to use.

As a special school there is no compulsion to have an RE lesson. However this is one of the most popular lessons on the timetable. There is never any question of writing as we sit in a circle with all the staff and students together. I might read a short story or an editorial from the tabloid press. I use as my source book *Frontiers* by Ralph Gower (published by Lion Books), a popular book for fifth years in mainstream schools. The questions we discuss on moral and religious issues are taken mainly from this book. After reading what I have prepared, and writing one or more questions on the board, anyone may say or ask anything relevant to the subject. As the weeks go by, everyone develops more and more confidence in asking questions and in trying to find answers. Often this lesson is quite daunting for new staff and they have to be encouraged to feel confident to speak. Sometimes they need the encouragement of the students who are used to this exchange of ideas.

In planning a curriculum that takes account of the perception our pupils have of themselves as young adults, we are also putting some responsibility on them to behave in an adult manner. If there is to be the opportunity to discuss important matters there must be self-discipline within the group. In a larger class the rules of discussion would have to be drawn up carefully with that class before starting on a controversial topic. I have found that if, initially, pupils have to repeat the last sentence spoken before adding their comment they listen more carefully and the discussion moves forward rather than being hi-jacked in different directions.

When there is a legal requirement to deliver the National Curriculum at Key Stage 4 there will not be the same opportunity to chose what to teach. Nevertheless it will still be important to consider carefully the methods of teaching what has been prescribed. I hope that there will be the opportunity to develop cross-curricular schemes which will engage the interest of all year 10 and 11 pupils.

Expulsion: the final sanction

Although some expulsions could, I am sure, be avoided if there were a more imaginitive curriculum for those who are giving cause for concern in years 10 and 11, a certain number of expulsions are probably inevitable.

Both the Warnock and the Elton Reports acknowledge the necessity of expulsions where the behaviour of one pupil is so out of control that the rest of the class cannot be taught. There is also a case for expulsion when dangerous and injurious behaviour is involved. There is no doubt however that some older pupils see expulsion during the final year at school as a reward, since it allows them to join the adult world of work a little earlier. Those who have little positive reinforcement of their increasing maturity in school are forced to seek it through defying the system. Not so long ago more fifth formers (now year 11 pupils) had the opportunity of taking office as school prefects. Many is the tearaway who had grown up overnight when given responsibility commensurate with his perception of himself as an adult.

Much of the behaviour which leads to expulsion can be seen as rebellion against keeping the same rules as the rest of the school. Those who have their progress in curriculum work marked with success rarely have the need to break rules as they obtain recognition legimately. The vandalism and aggression that forces suspension is often a manifestation of anger against a system that seems irrelevant to the young person. Sometimes the anger is directed against one teacher in particular. It is sometimes the very teacher whose own lack of confidence in the classroom prevents him or her from being able to recognise and acknowledge the adult in the young person in front of him or her. Sometimes anger is directed against the one teacher who is making a real effort to understand. For a number of complicated reasons dating back to their treatment as growing children, some young people are unable to accept overtures of friendship without putting them to the test. Only a very confident and self-assured teacher will be able to actually confront the young person with this as a possible explanation for their disruptive behaviour.

Perhaps some of the case histories described in Chapter 3 will help teachers to understand the factors that can lead up to the impossible behaviour of the young person who right now is making their lives miserable and preventing them from teaching those who wish to learn. We are not able to change what has gone before. We cannot blame ourselves for a set of circumstances that have been caused by agencies outside our control, nor may we be able to avoid a pupil being expelled. With some foresight in our curriculum work and the way we relate with younger children in the secondary school, however, we may be able to prevent individuals from reaching this stage.

Resources

Maths Games, the Highway Code game, World Link games and Checkmath are available from Taskmaster Ltd, Morris Rd, Leicester LE2 6BR

Journey through Britain, Journey through Europe, Train Journeys, Cross Country Hike and Map Jigsaws are in Arnolds Catalogue, Parkside Lane, Dewsbury Road, Leeds LS11 5TD.

CHAPTER 6

Examining Examinations

Although I have given examinations more than just a passing mention in earlier chapters, I feel the whole issue of examinations in the context of pupil behaviour is important enough to devote a whole chapter to it.

Who needs examinations?

In my role as an assessor for an examination board which enables adult learners to be credited with their efforts to improve their ability in communication skills, I am privileged to meet groups of adults who are trying to make up for what they see as missed opportunities at school. One centre is within a prison, where the men await my visit with nervous anticipation as they are so eager to receive their 'piece of paper'. None of them has ever before gained any kind of certificate. They leave me in no doubt that they feel it is important to have some kind of external examination certificate to show a prospective employer. Some of the prisoners admit that they truanted from school, or did not take any interest in their work. Others feel that they were not given enough encouragement by their teachers or were educated in special schools or units where no one did examinations. I am sure it is easier to say that examinations are not important than to actually believe it, particularly if you are the one who has none.

Among my other centres are one for pupils with moderate learning difficulties, another for adults trying to find a job after several years of unemployment and another for adults for whom English is a second language. There is absolutely no doubt that these three groups all prize highly the evidence that they have satisfied the demands of an external examining body. The teachers welcome me as a representative of the examination board and are eager to show me the innovative work they have produced in order to bring their specialised group to the required standard. Rightly or wrongly, external recognition seems to be as important to the staff as it is to the students.

I am not convinced that the examination certificate which accredits their elementary skills will necessarily give these candidates a better chance of employment, but I do think that the confidence and sense of achievement that it gives them will make them more likely to approach the search for a job positively and with a resilient attitude. I think it makes them feel better people and the award of a certificate, with the well-known logo of an external examining body, is personally significant to all these students.

The examination dilemma

Nevertheless, one of the most difficult decisions I have ever made in my work in the unit is to enter pupils for external examinations. Very often it is the fear of examinations, or the fact that the pupil has fallen behind with examination preparation in year 10, that has been one of the factors that has caused his referral to the unit. At one time I used to study the current syllabi of the examinations for which our pupils were being prepared but, in all but two cases, it was evident that these pupils had fallen so far behind that there was no prospect of their obtaining a pass grade. If these pupils were to obtain external accreditation it was clear that we would have to look outside the conventional examination boards. There was a fear, however, that if we found an examination that better met the needs of the students it would not be worth having since it would not be recognised by colleges and employers.

The local Further Education college entered mature returners for elementary RSA (Royal Society of Arts) examinations and offered to enter some of our pupils also. This appeared to meet our needs in terms of our pupils' levels of achievement, and it was also a recognised examination. We decided to prepare our pupils. However, despite the fact that they had all said that they wanted to do examinations, from the time they saw the papers our students' attendance deteriorated until it became evident that we could not risk entering them. As soon as this decision had been made, attendance returned to near normal although, ironically, students still expressed concern about not doing external examinations.

We went through all the same motions the following year. In that intake of pupils we had a rebellious girl who had been at a selective school. It was evident from her school report and the work she was doing that she was capable of tackling O Level GCE papers. Her headteacher was willing for her to return to take them and offered to lend us any books we might need; yet although her former teachers went to tremendous trouble to make sure she was provided with the work she needed, she steadfastly refused to do any homework and went missing from home during the vital time when the decision was being made to enter her for her examinations. Consistent with our experience the previous year, as soon as the time for the decision to enter her had passed, she reappeared and happily worked at a pace just ahead of the rest of the group for the rest of the year. Recently, at the age of 25, she came to tell me that now her two children have started school, she is studying for some of the examinations she 'did not have the chance to do at school'.

I became very frustrated at the way in which some of these pupils of average ability were saying that they wanted to do examinations and yet sabotaging every attempt I made to arrange this. I was also very conscious that many of their relatives had done extremely well in business with no formal qualifications at all. I became aware that, as teachers, most of us have had a specific type of education that is geared to examination success. It is therefore possible that we put too much emphasis on the gaining of paper qualifications and, in order to serve all our pupils, perhaps we should become more relaxed about the importance of examinations. After all, was it not important that we should make our pupils feel that they were OK as people with or without examination success?

With these pupils we had the dilemma that they had rejected, and been rejected by, the schools which focus so much of their work in the final two years on examinations, and yet they did not feel able to accept the alternative. Whatever attempts I made to minimise the importance of examinations, society made other noises. The 1980s were also the years of great public debate about the reforming of the examination system for school leavers – an exam for every pupil!

Examinations in control of the curriculum

The report produced by HMI (1978), *Truancy and Behavioural Problems in Some Urban Schools* had acknowledged many of the concerns I had about examinations and their effect on the education of many of our adolescents, particularly. From the outset we realised that any examinations we considered have to be relevant to a career in a trade, and must be available before the Easter leaving date:

> The greatest resistance to school came not from them [slow learners] but from those who were just above the border line of those qualifying

for [this] help. For them the transition to examination-based fully specialist teaching was unpalatable and irrelevant . . . . The malaise of the third year is in part an expression of adolescent confusion. For some young people this period of development can involve great additional stress . . . the search for personal identity and the need for close personal relationships, the crisis of examinations and the search for a vocational role. For those destined for semi-skilled work, the conventional approach to examinations holds little appeal . . . . In areas of high unemployment, even the fourth and fifth year interviews with careers officers can seem a little unreal, as do examination courses which culminate in the Summer Term for those who know they are leaving school at Easter (page 32).

In the findings of the Warnock Committee (DES, 1978) there is this statement which suggests that provision for maladjusted pupils,

> is not complete unless it affords educational opportunities of a quality which subsequently enables them to profit from further education and training on relatively equal terms with their contemporaries (11.61).

If our pupils are to profit from further education on *equal* terms with their peers then the colleges will want some proof that they are sufficiently literate and numerate to follow a recognised vocational course. I feel our search for an alternative to the conventional examinations is vindicated by Widlake (1983) when he observes how:

> Schools, being so heavily involved in certification, are bound to experience problems in devising programmes for pupils with special needs. The increasing disenchantment of some of these pupils provides the unanswerable case for some fresh approaches (p. 122).

Lowe (1988) says that:

> when a young person moves along that fatalistic path which ensures that he fails to achieve success, he receives very strong messages from significant people in his environment, that he is a failure. He then internalises this negative picture and we are left with a sad, despondent, underfunctioning youngster (p. 51).

I think it is clear from my description of pupils in Chapter 3 that, when deciding on examinations in our particular situation, all the considerations referred to in the extracts had to be taken into account. I am sure that anyone who has experience in teaching in a secondary school will recognise the pupils described here and their particular problems with the conventional examination syllabus. However, can pupils who are not prepared for examinations 'profit from further education and training on relatively equal terms with their contemporaries' (DES, 1978)?

Avoiding examination failure

In spite of motivational difficulties, when it came to the crunch pupils in the unit persisted in their request to be entered for examinations. We had to find a means of certification which was within their reach, but would also be recognised by employers and further education colleges, Most of our pupils had ambitions to gain trade qualifications. I was therefore delighted when I heard that the City and Guilds of London Institute (CGLI) had devised their own Foundation Course qualification for those students applying for admission courses leading to their trade qualifications but who did not have a minimum qualification in maths and English.

When we requested registration as a centre for the CGLI Foundation Course examinations in Numeracy and Communication Skills, we received welcome help and support from the assessor assigned to us, the Regional Chief Assessor, Belinda Singleton. That support has remained with us throughout the eight years that we have entered pupils for these qualifications. We were delighted to find a syllabus which could be adapted to our needs. Our pupils found the assignments relevant to their lives and well within their ability. It was good to find an examination where oral communication was considered as important as written communication. The ability to leave a clear message on an answerphone was seen as being as important as writing a short letter, and the ability to listen carefully to a message and pass it on accurately was considered as being as important as a reading comprehension. At that time Communications Skills comprised a course-work assessment and a multiple-choice paper. This was based on extracts from trade directories, car maintenance manuals, instruction books and other types of printed material that is encountered by most adults. Much of the material was in graphic form.

The Numeracy examination was a multiple-choice paper testing the kind of arithmetical problem that our pupils were likely to encounter in their daily working and home lives. We had the advantage of being able to link everything we taught to its practical application. Apart from their obvious relevance to everyday encounters I think the reason for the success of these examinations was the fact that our pupils found multiple choice very encouraging as they could always put something in the gap before handing in the paper. With the implementation of the National Curriculum the Secondary Examinations and Assessment Council (SEAC) decided that the City and Guilds Numeracy and Communication Skills examinations are not suitable for testing 16-year-olds. The CGLI has devised approved English and mathematics assessments that test the same attainments as the GCSE on three levels of competence. Although we had grave reservations in replacing Communication Skills with English, we have done so with considerable success.

Looking at GCSE as an examination for ALL

Why do we not do GCSE? After all, this is the examination which has broken down the barriers caused by GCE and CSE, and is designed to suit 80 per cent of the school population. At the time of writing the government has stated the intention that GCSE will be the main means of assessment at Key Stage 4, and that achievements at that stage will be graded on a scale 10–1 instead of on a scale A–G.

If pupils are proceeding well with course-work and keeping up-to-date with GCSE studies, it is very unlikely that they will be referred to us. For young people who lead supported, organised lives and are conscientious about completing their homework, the emphasis on cumulative accrediting of course-work has alleviated the strain of the examination. However, since 1989 one of the main reasons for referring pupils to us has been that they have fallen so far behind with their course-work that school has ceased to have relevance, since they already know that they have no chance of achieving a good grade in GCSE. In many cases they have been told that they will not be entered.

Many of the adolescents to whom I refer in this book do not have the settled and supported life-style necessary to consistently produce good course-work. Even in homes where there is a great warmth and concern for the children, there is not necessarily a suitable place for a teenager to do a considerable amount of homework, in peace and away from the distractions of family life. I was interested when, during a discussion about the 1990 examination results in my borough, a very perceptive councillor brought to the Education Committee's attention the fact that a vast number of children lived in homes where the accommodation comprised a through lounge-diner, usually dominated by the television set, a small kitchen with little working space and three bedrooms. He asked where, if there were more than two children in the home, were pupils expected to be able to do the amount of homework required by the GCSE. I sincerely hope that his suggestion to fund course-work centres in areas of high density housing is taken seriously. I am sure that this would make a difference for many children, especially if the centres were furnished with the kind of reference books and study aids which children in professional homes take for granted.

Rather than abandoning the idea of an examination which gives priority to course-work, I would like to see more effort being put into solving the problems of pupils who have an unequal chance because of home circumstances. Perhaps the initiative has to come from the examination boards in changing the type of course-work, or perhaps individual subject heads could, with the support of their local authority, make this fair for all pupils who are willing to make the effort.

Choosing the right examination

There is little doubt of the blow to their self-esteem that was caused by our pupils' removal from mainstream education. Most were aware that they had not completed enough course-work for their schools to enter them for the examinations. It was therefore of paramount importance that, if we were to enter them for examinations, we had to be fairly sure of success. We had also to make sure that we did not let the examinations become more important than the young person. Staff had to accept that even very able pupils might, for reasons of their own, not attend on the day of the examination, or refuse to finish the one piece of course-work required to reach a certain level.

We decided to plan a curriculum that was relevant and acceptable to young people on the verge of adulthood. Any examination which might be available would have to be flexible to fit in with our needs. I did not want to fall into the trap where the examination demands would rule our curriculum. The City and Guilds examinations had fulfilled all these criteria. Even when we no longer had access to Communication Skills we found the criteria for English were broad enough to be able to use the most useful of the Communication Skills assignments. Speaking and listening were still considered as important as reading and writing. We were agreeably surprised how well our pupils responded to the demand for a certain amount of creative writing, and how eagerly they used literature, especially poetry, as a stimulus for this.

The new maths criteria also added a fresh dimension to our maths teaching. The small group was ideal for work with investigations. This was a new approach for staff so in some cases the pupils were helping us, a fact which I think helped greatly in restoring their confidence. Many remembered these lessons in mainstream as times when they admitted they took advantage of the freer atmosphere in the room and wasted time.

The requirement for algebra was at first thought to be a problem but, because we spent some time talking about the applications of this skill, as well as recalling previous times when they had been faced with this work (see Chapter 5), initial problems were overcome and everyone achieved enough to fulfil the requirements of the first level. Some pupils became very enthusiastic and romped through the exercises to beyond the standard required for this examination. When they were told this they were both pleased and surprised, and it was at this point that several pupils started making tentative enquiries about college courses.

The investigations and the algebra were tackled purely because of the demands of the examination and, if we had stuck rigidly to our previous rule of a relevant curriculum, a number of our pupils would have missed a very rewarding and empowering experience. Nevertheless there were some who did not find the motivation to engage themselves in these two activities. For this small number we obtained permission to enter them for the well-established Numeracy examination. They were delighted to obtain passes in this at Level 1. Level 2 of this examination requires some knowledge of algebra and standard form. Although this group had resisted these topics before their success in Level 1, those who had gained credits or distinctions were very eager to grasp the nettle and learn these topics in order to pass the second level.

The greatest value of the examinations we have attempted has been that students have been able to gain tangible success early on in the course. This has led them to believe in themselves enough to make a real effort to reach a higher level. I think it is also important that with the City and Guilds English and maths examinations it is possible to guarantee a certificate for everyone. The candidate's enrolment lasts six months and so a student can have an attempt at Level 1 in December and Level 2 in March or May. They can, as long as sufficient course-work is completed at the appropriate level, enter two or three levels in the same series. Even if the examination is not passed, a course-work certificate will be issued. Course-work is split into short tasks and longer assignments. At least 70 per cent of the coursework criteria must be validated in the longer assignments which demonstrate the ability to use maths to solve everyday problems (e.g., decorating a room or running a charity event). If insufficient coursework is completed, it is possible to request a profile report for a student. The certificate issued is similar to the others and has a list of all the criteria in which the candidate has shown competence. This is available for English also, but in English there is no written paper.

A similar scheme is available for science, home economics, French, German, Italian and Spanish. We have not used these examinations yet but we are considering using the vocational French or German since there is as much credit for listening accurately as there is for speaking. There is acknowledgement of the fact that listening exercises are most valuable when spoken by a native speaker of the language. However, there is also recognition that it is possible to convey a message in a foreign language without perfect grammar, as long as the vocabulary is known. Obviously, the more correct the langue, the higher the level awarded, but a pass at a basic level shows that appropriate communication can be achieved in a working situation.

At present we also use Associated Examination Board basic tests which are widespread in units and popular in many schools. In their favour they are extremely cheap and easy to administer. They also provide a small unit the opportunity of a large range of subjects without risking a too great investment of time or money. I found the geography syllabus, in particular, broad and relevant. I felt that any school leaver should have learnt, during the course of 10 years at school, most of what was required for this paper. I was, however, disappointed to find that the general geographical knowledge of most of our pupils has, with a few noteworthy exceptions, fallen well short of the requirements. With only time for 40 minutes geography a week I have been discouraged by our extremely low pass-rate and have, with regret, decided to abandon this examination. Our pass rate has been better for health, hygiene and safety. Perhaps this is because we have 80 minutes each week for this. I have no doubts about retaining this examination as I think it has great relevance for the life of young people about to take their first jobs.

Difficulties with exams

Fear of failure

I am sure that few candidates enter examinations without some fear of failure. However, there are some pupils whose self-esteem is so fragile that they themselves fear damaging it in any way. There is no doubt that these are among our most troubled, and in some cases, our most troublesome adolescents. Deliberate disruption and overt bravado in class can be a means of avoiding failure. After all if a pupil causes enough disruption he or she is likely not to be entered for the examination, or to be removed from so many classes that he or she has a good excuse to either not turn up for the examination or to fail spectacularly. To work hard, and still risk failure, would be far more damaging to the self-esteem for these pupils.

Similar to these pupils are those who forget the day of the examination. They have been known to ring us just as the examination is finishing in order to ask if the examination is in the afternoon or tomorrow. All pupils are given their own personal timetables, and another is posted to their home during the week before examinations begin. If we have not seen a pupil for a few days we ring up the day before and remind them.

Fear of success

I find the fear of success more difficult to cope with than the more obvious fear of failure. Unfortunately, it is often our abler pupils who miss examinations. Susie was one of these. Had she remained in mainstream, despite poor attendance, I am sure she would have achieved several GCSEs with good grades. She was expected to pass all the AEB tests with credit. On the day before the exams she rang to say that the sister with whom she lived had been evicted from the house they occupied within walking distance from school. They were living in temporary accommodation the other side of the borough and there was no way that she would be able to obtain enough money for bus fares. I found out where she was living and immediately went there with the money to enable her to come to her first examination. I assured her that after each examination I would give her the means to return home and travel in again for the next one. Susie arrived for the first examination but disappeared minutes before I gave out the papers. I have not seen her since although I know she has been to the careers office to enlist their help in finding her a job. I sent her course-work certificates but she had not acknowledged them. Susie was a bright girl who had done well in school until she was 14. We later learnt that she had ceased to attend regularly as her younger sister had just reached the age of 9. This was the age at which Susie's step-father had started to abuse her and she was determined not to let this happen to her sister so she made sure she was always in the house when her sister returned from school. Susie's regard for herself was such that she would not allow herself to earn praise. If ever we admired a painting she did or a poem she wrote she would either spoil it or claim that another pupil had done it.

She was not alone among pupils who deliberately sabotaged their work. The first time we prepared for a course-work assessment we discovered, three hours before the assessor was due to arrive, that the best candidate's work had been torn up and scattered on the floor. We were very angry but, as we did not wish to provoke further incidents, we made no attempt to track down the culprit but set about ironing it and sellotaping it together again although Anna, the girl to whom it belonged, urged us not to bother. While we were doing this Robert, another very good candidate for whom we had also recommended a distinction, came in and said he knew we suspected him (we did, but we had not said so!), so he took his own work and tore up as much as he could before we intervened.

Although the assessor awarded distinctions to both these pupils on the strength of the work completed, Anna and Robert were adamant that they did not deserve it. Years later Anna admitted that she destroyed her own work because she thought the others in the community home where she lived would think she was 'showing off' if she had obtained a distinction. Robert now has a very responsible job in the Leisure Department of the borough, and I recently asked him why he had destroyed his work. He also said that, although a distinction would have pleased his very caring parents, it would have caused trouble among the friends he then had. Since then he has out-grown this feeling and has obtained good qualifications in further education.

Fear of boredom

When I did my survey of attitudes to examinations in special units I asked pupils to write down just five words that came to mind when they thought about examinations. A quarter of the respondents put down 'bored' or 'boring' as one of their words.

Although many of our pupils are eager to pass their examinations, as the day approaches they worry about whether they will be too bored if they have to sit there for two hours. They are always relieved when I tell them that they may leave the room after one hour if they have finished. Most pupils spend very little more than this minimum time in the room. It is not unusual for a candidate who has left the room early subsequently to complain that he did not reach a question near the end, which he now realises he could have done easily. Although half of the papers are multiple choice, and the others are questions requiring a word or sentence in answer, our pupils find it very difficult to sustain interest long enough to finish the paper.

I think that their addiction to smoking is one reason why many of our pupils find it difficult to remain in the examination room for two hours. As they leave the room and walk away from the building we see the inevitable column of smoke rise!

Conclusions

Can teachers in mainstream learn anything from our experience with examinations?

I know that we are in a very privileged position in being able to cater for individuals in a way that good teachers in mainstream can only dream about. However, I would like to see a more flexible attitude to the type of examination used. While I can see that GCSE is suitable for the majority of pupils, especially those with a settled home life with good facilities for homework, there is a small but significant minority of pupils for whom success in this examination is impossible. We have had a number of pupils referred to us as the end of year 10 because they have not done enough course-work to make a grade in GCSE a possibility. We hear about those pupils who are causing difficulties in schools because of their frustration. I know there are more who will simply drift away towards the end of year 11, or even remain and carry away with them a sense of futility and failure because they had no alternative to an examination which was not suitable to their circumstances. If they are lucky they might have a second chance of the kind of mentioned at the beginning of this chapter. Otherwise, they might carry this sense of failure through to their adult life and pass it on to their own children.

I know some schools use the AEB basic tests at the end of the fourth year. I feel they could well be used as a final examination for those who have not completed sufficient course-work. I would not like to see a return to the system where, when pupils arrived at the secondary stage, some were predestined for GCE and others for CSE from year 7. I welcomed the single examination for which all pupils could aim. Nevertheless, there are personal and emotional circumstances which can well occur in years 10 or 11 which prevent the completion of course-work or full involvement in the course. We run the risk of alienating the young person from education permanently if, at this stage, we cannot find some flexibility.

Exams for everyone?

From my experience with the pupils in the unit, and with mature students whose work I assess, I believe everyone should be given the opportunity to gain 'a bit of paper', if this is important to them. I have learnt a great deal from my small group of special adolescents about their feelings about examinations. At one time I went to great lengths to make sure that I only entered those who would pass, and I went to quite extraordinary lengths to make sure that everyone who was entered for an examination took their place in the examination room. I now enter everyone who asks to be entered. I have had some very pleasant surprises from those who have been determined to succeed and have, through determination and hard work, done so despite my gloomy prognostication. I make sure everyone knows their personal examination timetable and then I leave it to them to turn up. If a particularly good student fails to arrive for their examination I resist the temptation to go and fetch them. I now realise that there are a number of personal reasons that students may have for not doing an examination. In the end I must allow them the dignity of making their own decisions – even if they blame me for this later.

The future

For some years pupils have been taking from their schools a Record of Achievements – a carefully and methodically compiled record of all they have achieved academically, socially and athletically whilst they were at school. The difference between this and the old style school report has been the active participation of the pupil in compiling it. It also contains only positive statements which have been discussed and negotiated with the pupil. Where there has been an almost complete Record of Achievement, we have worked with the school to complete it for the young person. Unfortunately less than 10 per cent of our pupils have come with any Record of Achievement because so many of them were disaffected for months or even years before they came to us. Some had one or two changes of high school and records were not forwarded. Now that Records of Achievement are becoming an established part of year 11 certification I hope that they will be extended in a positive way to off-site provision. The profiles and certificates awarded by the City and Guilds are designed to fit into the Record of Achievement.

I will be interested to see if a scheme of accredited prior learning leading to National Vocational Qualifications (NVQs) will be available to us. There is a pilot scheme in a Cumbrian special school to accredit work experience in this way. Work experience is carefully chosen to make sure that each pupil has the opportunity to attempt to master as many of the competencies linked with an occupation as possible.

The National Council of Vocational Qualifications (NCVQ) sees paid employment as only one of the five areas of activity in which we work – the other four are home and family, study, voluntary work and leisure. The NCVQ is committed to recognising competence in all of these and to provide credit for them. If this lives up to its advance publicity it should be very empowering for those women who have formerly described themselves as 'just a housewife', and for those young people who, in periods of enforced unemployment, enter wholeheartedly into a sport. It should also encourage young people to have commitment to voluntary work if thereby they can gain qualifications which will be recognised by employers.

Employers' attitudes

In my survey, 32 of the 40 employers interviewed agreed that they would expect a young person to have some qualification in maths and English. Those who understand the difference between GCE and GCSE (mostly parents of teenagers themselves) said, with one exception, that they thought the latter examination was more helpful to employers as it showed that the young person was capable of working steadily throughout a two-year period. The one who favoured GCE felt that the standard of the new examination had been lowered 'so that everyone can pass'. Sixty per cent would only recognise a grade A–C as a pass. Of these only one said that he had no knowledge of the

City and Guilds examinations. The others said that they would consider these appropriate for young trainees.

Less than half had actually seen a Record of Achievement (May–July, 1990) but those who had felt it was very helpful. One employer added that he would also want to see some evidence in the form of examination certificates.

Although they all said that the way the young person looked and conducted him or herself at an interview was important, most convinced me that we should be helping our young people to gain some certificates to validate their 11 years in compulsory education. Many moderated what they said by remarking that it depended what the work was and if the young person wanted to progress in the firm. Most had an anecdote to relate about someone with no examinations, often illiterate, who had done well despite lack of success at school.

In conclusion I end, very much as I began, in saying that there is a time when most people feel they would like a piece of paper recognising their ability. It is important that they are given the opportunity to obtain this. However, it is also important never to put so much emphasis on examinations that one feels a failure as a human being without them. The new Records of Achievement and NVQs should allow more school leavers to feel that they have a good chance of success in life.

CHAPTER 7

Exceptional Solutions to Exceptional Problems – In or Out of School?

At the beginning of this book I stated that the disruptive behaviour of some adolescents was by no means a new problem. However, perhaps the special solutions that have evolved during recent decades have caused this problem to seem more exceptional.

The rise and fall of the off-site unit

The 1970s was a decade of spectacular growth in the number of off-site units which were set up for pupils whose behaviour was no longer tolerated in mainstream schools. The majority of these units were for pupils during their last two years of compulsory schooling, although there was also some provision for much younger children. The units were additional to the increased amount of provision for those who had already been diagnosed as maladjusted or educationally subnormal (terms still in use in the 1970s when the emphasis was still on handicap rather than need). The strength of the off-site unit, as far as school administration was concerned, was that pupils could be consigned to a unit swiftly, and with a minimum of procedure. It could be done on the advice of the head, with little consultation among teachers or other workers in education.

My unit was one of those 'born' as a result of perceived crisis in the mid-1970s. In common with other similar units described in Chapter 2, it came to maturity in the 1980s. After a number of moves it established a permanent base and became part of the accepted educational provision. Schools realised that they had to bid for places early if they wished to transfer their pupils as the places were filled earlier and earlier each year. The admission procedure was tightened up, with referral only possible if approved by one of the authority's psychologists. From early experience in the unit, I had found that those who came into the unit at the beginning of year 10 or the end of year 9 became bored in this very restricted environment and drifted away early during year 11. I therefore made the decision not to take any pupil who had more than a year of schooling left. I would like to think that this meant that schools tried to contain their younger pupils for a few months longer. However, I know four or five every year spent much of year 10 on home tuition, with the expectation that they would come to the unit as soon as they were able.

Although in the early days of off-site units the emphasis seemed to be on pastoral care with a curriculum based on social skills, by the 1980s the need for a fuller curriculum was being acknowledged by many units. With the implementation of the National Curriculum, the teaching staff in units tried hard to find some way to cover as many subjects as possible in order to be seen to be working in the spirit of the new requirements.

From the onset of the 1990s these casually conceived off-site units have received closer scrutiny than ever before. This has been partly as a result of the change of method in funding education. Off-site units have had to be seen to be worth their share of the 'central money', especially in authorities that have wanted to maximise delegation of funds under Local Management of Schools (LMS). The concerns of authorities have not been wholly financial however, but largely influenced by the Warnock Report's (DES, 1978) recommendations that, with few exceptions, pupils should remain in mainstream provision.

The Elton Report (DES, 1989) acknowledged a need for some special provision for those whose behaviour had an exceptionally harmful effect on the education of others, but stated regret that the teachers who had taught for some years in units had not had any influence on finding strategies for helping these pupils in mainstream schools. It recognised the fact that 'Alternative provision has often been developed piecemeal by LEAs as needs have been perceived' (p. 156). The Report goes on to recommend that LEAs should review their provision for difficult pupils, taking full account of:

> the need to provide adequate, appropriate and cost-effective support for schools and individual pupils;
> the importance of keeping pupils in, and if they are removed, returning them to mainstream wherever possible;
> the balance between the inherent disadvantage of off-site units and the need to maintain a minimum number of off-site places;
> the benefits that can accrue from the work of support teams in mainstream schools with access to on-site units; and

the need to ensure that support teams are adequately resourced to carry out their work effectively (sections 53.1-5).

In common with many other similar units, mine is being replaced by a service whereby provision is directly linked to the needs and interests of individuals, rather than offering a similar programme to a group with very diverse aims and difficulties.

What has segregating pupils in units achieved?

I have no doubt at all that there are pupils who have attended units and achieved far more than they would have done in mainstream provision. Much of the literature on special units concentrates on the needs of the troublesome or disruptive pupil, but I think that perhaps it has been the troubled pupil, the pupil who has suddenly failed to thrive in his or her mainstream school, who has been most able to 'grow' again in a smaller unit. Yet while I am sure that most of the most troublesome pupils have been referred to us by the schools, I think we have only had a few of the troubled adolescents, mostly those who have also displayed disruptive or unusual behaviour in class. One very troubled girl was only identified as having problems when she attended school from time to time wearing a surgical collar discarded by another member of the family. Those who did not act out in any way were only identified if they had teachers who were sensitive enough to realise that they needed extra help. These pupils do not cause a management problem at school, or pose a threat to teachers, and so are less likely to be referred to units.

When ex-pupils, who have had a troubled and stormy adolescence, cross the street to tell me that they have not been 'in trouble' for a couple of years, that they are doing well at work, that they are buying their own house, that they have completed their college course, that their children are doing well at school and to relate other personal successes, I am pleased that they realise this matters to me. I also wonder if this would have happened whether there had been intervention during their final year at school or not. As Topping (1983) states, we have no way of knowing if there would have been a spontaneous remission from unacceptable behaviour in any case.

Almost certainly we succeeded with these pupils because of the way in which we worked. Of course, mainstream teachers would be right to point out that we are able to work in a more individual, personal way because we had a much more favourable staff: pupil ratio; and because of our relatively isolated position we could also afford a low key response to some disruptive behaviours until trust and respect had been gained.

The effect of units on mainstream education

What effect have we had on mainstream schools? With the arrival of the 'unit', did disruptive behaviour in the classroom cease to be a problem? Can we be sure that other pupils' education has benefited by the removal of 'disruptive' pupils? Have other pupils conformed because of fear of banishment to 'the unit', when others of their more recalcitrant class-mates have disappeared thence? Those of us who have spent much of our careers developing these short-lived units would like to hear a resounding 'yes' to all these questions, but we know this is not true. Indeed, in some respects the spread of units may have worsened the situation.

Unfortunately the very existence of units has led to certain children being given a disruptive label and being seen as problems to be solved outside the school. Whilst there are children who bring their problems into school with them, I feel that, before the proliferation of units, there have always been teachers in the schools who are skilled at helping these children. Sometimes this is by informal counselling, especially in the case of very experienced teachers who had spent a number of years in the same neighbourhood. Often special adaptations can be made to the curriculum in order to motivate a reluctant pupil to engage him or herself in work instead of disruptive behaviour. I can remember a wise head of fourth year, in the 1960s, arranging for a particularly troublesome group of girls to help in the nursery class of the adjoining primary school provided they completed the English and maths work that they were set and behaved in a reasonable manner in the school.

There is no doubt that, if there is widespread closing of units, schools will have to devise ways of adapting their teaching to suit some of the children whom they are not at present engaging. Part of this will concern the curriculum, but another important factor will be teaching style. Included in teaching style will be the way in which the teacher interacts with the young person. Those teachers with experience in units should now be encouraged through INSET work, to share their experience and skills with those who have not had the same opportunity to work closely with difficult and damaged adolescents.

Curriculum issues

The final pronouncements on the curriculum for Key Stage 4 will be important for children with behavioural problems. In its original form it was evident that only a limited percentage of our year 10 and 11 pupils would be able to cope with ten subjects to GCSE Level. Even without music, art and PE it was clear that the sheer volume of facts to be learnt and criteria to be met would place too heavy demands on both teachers and taught. Those of our pupils who came to us via the 'remedial' class or 'home tuition' often complain that they did nothing but English and maths for the year before they came to us. At one time we did little but these basics. With the National Curriculum, there will now be an obligation to *offer* a full curriculum to every child. This can be nothing but an improvement for those who were deemed to be worthy of only a very narrow curriculum, a criticism also levied against special schools before the Warnock reforms placed them under closer scrutiny.

One of the reasons for adolescents being both troubled and troublesome in school is the feeling of failure and there is a danger of the National Curriculum increasing this problem. For example, if a young person has reached the age of 15 and finds lessons in modern languages a cause of acute embarrassment and frustration, then nothing is to be gained from insisting on a further year of the same. Yet the answer to this problem might not be to abandon the subject. If a modern language must be done, try a different one to survival level. There are a number of courses, designed for adult beginners, which are available on audio and video tape at most resource centres. In one school I was in, the head of modern languages invited anyone who was interested to come and learn Spanish with him at lunch times. A number of pupils whose families had booked holidays on the 'Costas' went along and were surprised to find that the teacher was as much a beginner as they were. He had recorded 'Digame!' from BBC Television and Radio. Pupils happily bought the attractive and reasonably priced text book that accompanied the series. Surely a similar exercise would satisfy the requirement to learn a modern language for Key Stage 4 pupils and be a learning experience for everyone.

I have already suggested ways of adapting the curriculum to prepare for alternative examinations which will ensure that the pupil feels successful (see Chapter 6). Whatever is said about all grades in GCSE being pass grades, few pupils will be proud of seven or eight F grade passes.

Another problem concerns the danger of the overloaded Key Stage 4 curriculum crowding out the traditional practical subjects such as wood work and metal work because of the different demands of the Design and Technology syllabus. If we wish to engage non-academic students at this stage, we will have to make sure that these traditional craft subjects remain available. These young people are preoccupied more than ever with the necessity of having some skill to offer an employer. There is nationwide concern about the 'skills gap' which renders so many of our young people unemployable unless they are willing to do training. It is unfortunate that LMS has also caused the demise of Link courses at Further Education Colleges in some authorities, as the money previously allocated to these courses has become part of the schools' delegated budget. Some pupils who were not succeeding in the school classroom were motivated by being in an environment which recognised their incipient transition to adulthood and where the rules were geared to adolescents rather than children.

Work experience can be very valuable in helping reluctant pupils to understand how the work which they are doing at school relates to the world of employment. However, in some schools the opportunity to do work experience has first to be earned by acceptable behaviour, reliable punctuality and attendance. This is understandable in view of the difficulty of finding enough placements for every pupil. It is unfortunate, however, that this often penalises the very pupils that work experience might best motivate.

Classroom communication

I would like to see much more emphasis on understanding adolescent development in training courses for secondary teachers. This is probably the time that even skilled and caring parents find their children most difficult to understand. It is the time when the young person is desperate to be recognised as an adult but, in many other ways, still has many infant needs. This is especially so in the case of many of the more difficult pupils with whom we are faced each day.

Some of the case histories related in Chapter 3 demonstrate evidence of adolescents facing unfulfilled infant needs, especially in the case of children who have been burdened with adult responsibilities and decisions from a very early age. Even when an adolescent is in a caring family with adults who are able to take appropriate roles, there is often a degree of confusion as development is uneven and unpredictable with the approach of puberty and the commencement of intense feelings towards other people. In a household where the adults are still battling with unfulfilled infant needs, and still engaging in fresh sexual liaisons, the degree of confusion and the amount of support needed from outside is likely to be much more. Some troubled adolescents may find a stable person in their family or neighbourhood who will help them through the inevitable crises of this stage. For others the teacher at school is often the most stable adult they know. Because the relationship between teachers and the taught cannot easily imitate that between parent or confidant and child this can cause additional frustration. Pupils in the unit have often told me how rude and unkind they were to the teacher who tried hardest to help them. One girl, who later disclosed to me that she had been sexually abused, explained that she had wished to tell her teacher but 'there were always others there'.

I am not suggesting that, in addition to everything else, teachers should make themselves into second parents for their pupils. However, I think it might help teachers to cope if they realise that sometimes it is *because* they relate well to their pupils that they are recipients of the anger those pupils would like to feel safe enough to express to their parents. If teachers can manage not to take the rudeness of pupils personally, but have time to discuss it after the heat of the moment has passed, it is sometimes possible to reach that child and key into ways of engaging him effectively in the lesson. There is a real fear among teachers that this approach could look like weakness, as if you are afraid to challenge the rebellious youngster. However, any experienced teacher knows that an immediate verbal rebuke to an angry adolescent is more likely to provoke further trouble. Better to make a quiet acknowledgement of displeasure, coupled with a firm refusal to waste lesson time in pursuing the matter, and then make a point of following this up (e.g., at change of lesson) to put into words what has happened, in a calm way, so that it is clear that is is the deed and not the pupil that you dislike.

I think it is important to be aware when working with sensitive adolescents that they often find it threatening to be in close physical proximity to an adult. The caring gesture of a hand placed on the shoulder can be resented as an invasion of personal space, or misinterpreted as an unwelcome advance. When you talk to an adolescent about his or her behaviour, it is easy to interpret their refusal to face you and their sullen reaction as insolence rather than embarrassment. Few adolescents are able to surrender in any way when 'pushed into a corner' because of a misdemeanour. It may be sometime later that you learn that he or she was listening, and did take notice of what was said. It is very important never to place the adolescent into an humiliating position because of determination to provoke some respectful response. If the pupil is humiliated then he or she will carry that to the next lesson, and beyond. If instead, because of the entrenched position of the youngster, it is the teacher who is humiliated, it will become more difficult for him or her to cope with that class and maybe even the next one.

Humiliation can take place very easily in the classroom. I have witnessed pupils being deliberately asked questions they cannot answer in order to 'cut them down to size'. This is unforgivable, and yet I have heard it justified by the suggestion that 'it keeps them on their toes'. I know of a large, ungainly 13-year-old girl who has been unable to face going into school since being called out in front of the class to write her spellings on the board. I do not know what the teacher hoped to achieve by this act of humiliation as she knew the girl not only had problems in spelling but was easily embarrassed, and had difficulty in making and keeping friends. For a very few pupils this might make them do learning homework that they would otherwise neglect; but it could destroy the confidence and self-esteem of others who might need help in learning, and experience unsuitable conditions for homework.

A good teacher will know where to direct certain questions without putting a child into a situation where he or she can be ridiculed. In a mixed ability class it is often possible to ask questions that are open-ended enough to be safely answered on a number of levels. The immediate and simple response of a less able pupil might provide the springboard for a more sophisticated answer from an able child, which leads to discussion in which all abilities can join. Differentiation should not mean that while some of the class are engaged in an exercise which involves looking up texts and writing essays, others are very obviously filling in time completing and colouring a work-sheet. Some care can be taken to offer open-ended assignments that pupils of all abilities can do side by side and determine their own level of response. If pupils are to work in groups it is important to make sure that the child who is less able is not simply a passenger in an able group. Although outwardly this pupil might seem to be happy to allow the others to do all the work, he or she will be internalising more hurt and frustration, and losing what little motivation he or she still has.

Adolescents often find it very difficult to express their feelings of frustration and anger to the appropriate people. A pupil who seems to revel in doing the least work possible and copying homework in the playground might well feel very angry and frustrated that he or she needs to do this. As year 10 and the spectre of public examinations approaches this pupil feels more and more frustrated by his or her inability to cope and yet can only rarely ask for help. This is the age at which peer group pressure is at its height and if the child is part of a group within which prowess at school is not admired, then it becomes more difficult for the pupil to seek help.

What can the teacher do about this? It is important not to take the child's nonchalance about his or her inability to cope with the curriculum at face value. With most children it is possible to point out to them their strengths and find a way to build on them. Sometimes underachievers need help to sort out priorities if they have fallen a long way behind. They need to be shown that they have not been written off and it is still important to the teacher that they feel OK in class. The individual pupil might be unable to respond to this. In my experience, most pupils will respond to quiet, positive intervention from teachers who evidently care about them as people, unless they have deep-rooted problems outside school. Intervention at this stage is a better investment of time than spending it later dealing with disruptive behaviour when the frustrated pupil becomes disaffected from his or her work in the classroom.

Teachers as counsellors?

There is undoubtedly a role for heads of year and form teachers as unofficial counsellors for some very troubled children. Unfortunately, although many teachers have the skills necessary, few have the training or support that they need if they are to take on this responsibility. For many children it is important to have someone who will *listen* to them. For some teachers it is quite difficult to resist the temptation to interrupt the flow with advice. It is important that the child can finish without interruption. If there is a pause it can be useful to give back to the child what he or she has said, in a way that shows that you are listening and what he or she is saying does matter to you. This is especially important if the time you can give that child is already running out. It might be necessary to decide whether you will invite the child to come and talk to you again or whether you should suggest he or she seeks more expert help. It is important that anything disclosed that might have to be taken further is first discussed between the two of you. However, it is not constructive to start discussing this if the next class is already outside the door! It is important that a time to return is arranged. This commitment must be kept and the pupil will be more at ease if at the outset he or she knows how long you will be able to talk without interruption.

Adolescents rarely have the chance to talk to adults in this way, and, if they have very urgent need of this kind of response, they often delay until the last possible moment the most important thing they want to say. If it is a matter that could be helped with support from elsewhere it is important that the child knows who else will be involved. This prevents the child being anxious whenever he or she sees the counsellor talking to another adult. If it has been important enough for the child to seek adult help it must on no account be dismissed as trivial or a waste of time. The trust of these adolescents is fragile and easily destroyed.

There are some adolescents who will approach a sympathetic member of staff repeatedly with what seem to be trivial problems. Cynics may dismiss this as an attempt to obtain special attention. Nevertheless there could be a really important problem that he or she is not ready to disclose until he or she has tested the possible response and has begun to feel trust. If his or her requests are treated in a business-like fashion, making sure that he or she does not miss or arrive late for lessons, he or she might eventually be able to speak about the underlying problem, or they may stop coming since he or she has satisfied their need for attention. The need for attention could be a frustrated infantile need at a time when there are events in the family which are taking away any attention which the pupil has previously enjoyed at home.

No teacher should ever feel forced into the role of counsellor as this is a skilled and time-consuming role. Although it is a role which I have enjoyed throughout my career, there have been two periods of personal crisis when I have felt unable to help pupils in this way. I think it is important to recognise these times and be able to put the child in touch with an adult who is strong enough to help them. I am confident that if teachers who have a natural ability for this work were given an opportunity for in-service training and released from some of their timetable demands to counsel pupils, much of the undoubted advantages of the off-site unit would be found in schools.

Although I advocate release from timetable commitments I am thinking in terms of flexibility in starting and ending the day. I think that school counselling can lose much of its value if pupils miss lessons in order to spend time with the counsellor. Proper counselling of troubled adolescents can be a very empowering exercise since the young person is helped to make his or her own informed decisions. They learn how to approach a problem from a number of angles, prioritise and choose a solution. This can leave them with a positive skill which will be invaluable to them as young adults.

Whole-school discipline policies

Although I have always enjoyed the challenge of trying to engage the most difficult pupils in work that will lead them to a feeling of success, I have always had misgivings about gathering all the most potentially difficult 15- and 16-year-olds under one, rather isolated, roof. At worst it could turn them into recognised outcasts, unfit to be educated alongside other young people. At best, even if they benefit from a more suitable curriculum and good, individual teaching, they will have to explain to every prospective employer why they finished their education at an off-site unit.

I welcome the move towards schools making a conscious effort to review their discipline policies to prevent disruptive behaviour by positive means. INSET money invested in training key members of staff to run whole-school discipline policies is well spent. Rutter (1979) highlighted the difference certain schools could make to pupils' education, showing how the ethos of the school made a difference to its effectiveness. It was one of the first attempts to lay responsibility for difficulties in school at the door of the school instead of on ineffective parenting, poor environment and home problems.

Forming a whole-school discipline policy should not be seen as the exclusive task of the senior management team, but they have an important part to play at the outset. There are recommendations to gather data on what is actually happening in the classroom and other areas which cause concern before the staff can begin to plan in a systematic manner. In this way it is possible to pin-point areas of the school, times of the day, days of the week, and the particular lessons where an above-average number of incidents take place. After these data are collected it is possible to have a more constructive meeting with the staff, since discussion will be based on fact and situation rather than personalities and isolated incidents.

It is important that whoever leads or facilitates the discussions leading to a whole-school discipline policy is skilled at enabling poeple to feel at ease and not threatened by each other. There are many teachers who feel too vulnerable to admit that there are any parts of the day or week when they are uneasy about discipline. It is important to create as much coherence as possible in the staff team. This can occur if everyone feels that they are party to the facts and on an equal footing in the decision-making. It may be constructive to ask small groups of staff to work on particular issues. In this context it is easier for the more vulnerable to discuss their own experiences. Sensitivity is important when asking established staff to accept a change in the way of working and it is important that they should feel part-ownership of whatever decisions are made.

Every area of the school will be looked at and it will be important to find out how pupils feel about the areas of the school and the school day that are causing concern. If it is not possible to involve pupils directly, feed-back from the pastoral staff could be the next best thing. When planning the rules by which the school will operate it is important that they are kept to a manageable number and positively phrased to indicate the expected rather than the unwanted behaviour. It is also important that discussion takes place about whether they are negotiable, and under what circumstances, and at what stage they can be reviewed. If there are too many rules and they are applied with total rigidity they can be used as a weapon against staff who become so fixated on the implementation of the rules that lesson time is lost while battles are fought over one rule. However, if there is such flexibility that exceptions are often made, there will be confusion and subjectiveness creeps in, with some teachers being labelled 'soft' by pupils or colleagues. Even in a unit for pupils who have been unable to conform to the rules at their schools, there has always been an acknowledgement of the fact that rules are necessary for a group of people to be comfortable sharing the same premises.

In the process of forming a whole-school policy it will be important to look carefully at both curriculum and timetable. It is sometimes helpful to adapt either one of these, or both, in order to prevent certain groups clashing in certain areas at identified 'difficult' times of the week. Different days have been identified by different researchers as being more likely to bring discipline problems. Friday afternoon will immediately come to mind. Very few off-site units function on a Friday afternoon.

It might be necessary for teachers to acknowledge that they need to improve identified skills to prevent having difficulty with certain classes. For example, mixed-ability teaching needs skills that many teachers, especially those who have come to a comprehensive school after years in a grammar school, have not been taught. The coordinator of the subject or the special needs coordinator may be able to give some tactful help in differentiating work so that every pupil in the class feels valued and successful.

For some pupils who find it difficult to commit themselves to one subject for a sustained period, the introduction of a modular curriculum in years 10 and 11 might help. If each module only lasts half a term no one has to engage a difficult group of youngsters beyond the limit of their concentration. They are also able to see themselves building up a collection of credits in each module which, if carefully planned, should result in covering their course-work as painlessly as possible.

If such arrangements were only available to the lower achievers, however, it could devalue the modular curriculum. This could also mean that certain subjects, along with the staff who taught them, were seen to have less status than others. Just as streaming tends to create an underclass which can seek to gain a reputation of being disruptive, so some options come to be seen as available to the academic pupils while others, notably practical subjects, are seen to be for the less able. This can cause classes to be overweighted with the pupils whose self-esteem is such that they feel an obligation to provide the entertainment for the class. Perhaps more encouragement for higher achieving pupils to accept the challenges of practical subjects would redress the balance here.

In looking at improving the discipline in a whole school it is important to look at ways of making every single pupil and adult feel valued. The physical appearance of the building is important in this respect. Even if it is necessary to use 40-year-old pre-fabs tagged on to an old building, it is important that everywhere is kept clean, any graffiti is wiped off as soon as it appears, broken furniture is repaired and the walls are regularly repainted. There is no doubt that carpeted areas cut down on jarring noise and are more pleasant to work in.

The process that leads up to the formation of a whole-school discipline policy encourages all staff to look at the environment, the timetable and the curriculum in a way they have never done before. The process of forming a school policy will develop out of awareness of the factors which aid good working discipline.

Outreach

Whereas the whole-school policy of managing pupil behaviour is developed by those within the school, Outreach involves trying to provide within-school behavioural support from outside. As the findings of the Warnock Report forced special educationists to look carefully at their function in the light of the increased integration of pupils with special needs into mainstream, many started to consider the support they could give the schools who were learning to deal with these pupils who had been traditionally consigned to special schools. An increasing number of advertisements for posts in remaining special schools have mentioned 'Outreach work in local schools' as part of the duties and skills required.

Some authorities have formed 'Outreach Teams' of teachers recruited especially to work alongside colleagues in schools to help them to find strategies for containing and engaging pupils who could otherwise be heading for exclusion and placement in an off-site unit. The teachers recruited in these teams have usually had proven success in dealing with difficult pupils in a special school or unit for emotionally and behaviourally disordered children. As well as being skilled teachers and managers of difficult children, in this role they must be tactful and perceptive communicators, able to diagnose the problem in a classroom and help a teacher to solve it without any loss of that teacher's confidence and self-esteem. Many teachers who trained before the 1980s have found it difficult to become accustomed to sharing the classroom with a learning support teacher. The idea of being observed in action by an 'expert' in behaviour can make even an experienced teacher feel very vulnerable.

There has been an Outreach team in Leicester city for more than a decade. Pupils who give cause for concern in schools are often referred during their last year in the primary school. The head of the service, and one of the team teachers who is attached to the secondary school to which the child will go, attends a multi-disciplinary meeting to discuss the problems and decide on what level of intervention will be needed. Everyone involved in the child's life will be represented at this meeting – parents, social worker, Education Welfare Officer, GP, probation officer and occasionally a youth leader if the youth club plays an important part in the child's life. It might be decided that it would be helpful if a third party were readily available if either the child or one of his or her teachers feels that difficulties are arising. The Outreach teacher has regular contact with the parents and is therefore in a position to know if there is anything going on at home which might be responsible for difficulties at school. An added advantage of this system is that, since there is not a specific number of places available, there is no temptation to refer pupils in order to fill existing places. Another advantage is that the strategies agreed can often have useful overspill effects which benefit other pupils too.

In Outreach programmes, every effort is made to keep the pupil in mainstream school and to provide appropriate support for the staff as the need arises. With disruptive pupils in years 10 and 11 work experience may be arranged in an attempt to keep the young person out of areas of conflict and to add relevance to the curriculum. Because of difficulties of control at home, staff also arrange some work experience during the holidays so that the pupils' lives retain some of the structure of term time.

Despite the efforts of a very able and well-established team, some pupils in Leicester are excluded from school in the final year. A programme is devised which includes some work experience, sessions at a local FE College if there is sufficient motivation, and some teaching in the 'home tuition' unit.

In Brighton there is a similar system where outside intervention is successfully being used to support the education of troubled and troublesome adolescents in mainstream schools. The teachers in this scheme work very closely with the schools to help teachers to engage these pupils as successfully as possible in the curriculum. All pupils are in school for at least 10 per cent of the time. Some, although on the books of the project, are in school for 100 per cent of the time, but they and their teachers know that there is someone who knows the situation and will be available if there are difficulties. Some pupils come out of school on one or two days a week to undertake work experience which is arranged by the team. As well as appropriate alternative courses, there are two 'club' sessions a week. This is a session when, under the guidance of project staff, youngsters play table tennis, snooker or board games in an informal setting. Attendance at a club session can be a carrot which keeps the youngster in school for the rest of the week. The important difference between this and the units described in Chapter 2 is that pupils go to the unit for a specific purpose, not for containment. They are not banned from their secondary school but, on the contrary, have to attend for at least two sessions a week. Whilst they are in school they are expected to conform to the expectations of that school.

These are just two of a number of such schemes. In the London area of Tower Hamlets there is a well-documented scheme that has reached maturity, having been founded in the late 1970s; this is described fully by Coulby and Harper (1985). The authors describe work with primary-age children as well as those in secondary schools. In each case the school retains full responsibility for the pupil. Unfortunately absence, a manifestation of continuing disaffection, is often a cause for concern on such projects, especially towards the end of year 11, despite intervention being tailored to the needs of individuals as far as possible.

The authority for which I work is in the process of replacing the off-site unit with a 'Year 11 Project', the aim of which is to design individual programmes for young people based on their declared interests and enthusiasms. Originally it was decided that there would be no compulsion for young people in the project to do the traditional basic subjects of English and maths. It was decided that if they felt later that they needed to do this because of the expectations of employers, they could do it after they left. The intention was for the youngsters to spend most of their time on work experience, backed up by suitable college courses. However, among the eight pupils who have been interviewed for the project at time of writing, both parents and pupil in each case have expressed, as a priority, a desire to gain a qualification in maths and English. As a consequence of this, courses have been arranged leading to City and Guilds Certificates. Eliciting an interest or enthusiasm from these pupils has proved more difficult, and we have found ourselves leading with suggestions from what we have been told about the pupil. It will be sometime before we know if this approach is going to be successful. There will, doubtless, be an evolutionary period of trial and error before the project reaches the maturity of the Leicester project. I hope that it will grow 'downwards' into the schools to provide Outreach intervention rather than reaction to crisis.

Transitional difficulties

Many teachers in units which are closing are wondering if they will be able to use the experience they have gained if they returned to mainstream in a support role. The Elton Report (DES, 1989) supports this possibility for those who have devised strategies for giving reluctant and defensive pupils self-confidence, and for engaging these same pupils in cognitive aspects of the curriculum. There will be difficulties for many teachers who have spent most of their careers in a unit environment in adapting to work in mainstream education. They will have to approach their role with a degree of humility as they will soon realise that there are other market-driven priorities in a mainstream school. In the staff-room pecking order, the teacher who can claim three figure GCSE and A level success in his or her subject stands higher than the teacher who has managed to squeeze two pieces of course work out of a reluctant member of the lowest year 10 group.

There may also be a degree of hostility from those who, dismayed at not being able to recommend the removal of a disruptive pupil to the off-site unit feel positively threatened at having to teach their classes in front of another teacher. Offering advice and support in these situations will have to be done with great diplomacy and tact, dwelling on any strengths that may have been evident in the lesson before suggesting strategies for the named pupil. It might be evident that the main problem is not the pupil but the layout of the classroom, the materials used or the pace of the lesson. Changing any of these will have to be handled with kid gloves and a willingness to be very patient in reaching one's aim, but a successful outcome should benefit all pupils and not only the troublesome ones.

Adolescents with problems are often very quick to pick up and exploit any tension between significant adults in their environment. The Outreach teacher will have a role where he or she is working for the good of both the teacher and the pupil, but gaining the confidence of one could mean alienating the other unless there is an attempt to make both feel responsible for any improvement that occurs. There is no room for an Outreach teacher who wants to be seen as the one who can manage the pupils better than their timetabled teachers. If Outreach is working properly the subject teachers should feel empowered by their increasing confidence in dealing with pupils whose behaviour has previously been too challenging for the classroom.

Conclusion

Schools cannot use the difficulties of children's background and home lives as an excuse for failing to look carefully at their own curriculum and practice to see if improvements can be made. There is, however, a small percentage of pupils who are genuinely troubled by factors beyond the control or understanding of the school. Many of these pupils are quiet and seem to be functioning adequately in mainstream school. Often the first time they come to the notice of teachers is when they are persistently absent. Now that there is an emphasis on course-work these pupils are emerging as those falling behind with this demand.

It is only since the inception of GCSE exams that these troubled children have been referred to the unit in numbers equalling their more troublesome peers. Previously they were only referred if a highly perceptive form teacher realised that they were struggling with other problems. In the safe environment of the unit, with the same group of staff for all lessons, these pupils have been able to talk about the troubles that are making it difficult for them to concentrate on anything else. A few have carried the secret of sexual abuse with them for much of their school life; most have disclosed a catalogue of bereavement, family illness, rejection, poverty, fear of eviction, fear of physical abuse and premature adult responsibilities. This is a fact of life. Rarely would intervention from an outside agency at this stage be appropriate unless requested by the youngster. However, unit staff are experienced and have the time to help the adolescent to make some kind of sense of what has happened and to work out methods of coping and initiating some change. Added to this, help to validate the previous 11 years of school by gaining some examination certificates can often make this particularly depressed child feel more able to cope with the transition from school to working life.

There is no doubt that much disruptive behaviour is an expression of anger against injustices elsewhere, and can be a depressed pupil's device for attracting the kind of censure which he or she feels they deserve. A common factor in many of those whose behaviour is disruptive in class is a lack of self-esteem. These pupils rarely display disruptive behaviour in the unit since the emphasis is always on identifying strengths and building on them. These particular pupils who are identified because of their troublesome behaviour can often gain much from an individual programme designed to build self-esteem.

Whether all children are educated in mainstream or whether there is a miscellany of special schools, units, centres and projects, there will always be pupils who are troublesome in the classroom, and those whom we may not notice so easily, but who are very troubled. Equally there will always be teachers who will rise to the challenge and have a real desire to help these children to succeed in education. I believe there is a tremendous wealth of experience and expertise in working sensitively and thoughtfully to make school a happy and enabling experience for these pupils. What is important is that teachers share with each other successful strategies, and are united in their aim to help pupils to feel fulfilled and empowered by their 11 years in compulsory education.

Bibliography

Bell, P. and Best, E. (1986) *Supportive Education*, Oxford: Blackwell.

Benyon, J. (1985) *Initial Encounters in the Secondary School*, London: Falmer Press.

Charleton, T. and David, K. (1990) *Supportive Schools*, Basingstoke: Macmillan Educational.

Coleman, J. (1980) *The Nature of Adolescence*, London: Methuen & Co.

Coulby, D. and Harper, T. (1985) *Preventing Classroom Disruption, Policy, Practice and Evaluation in Urban Schools*, Beckenham: Croom Helm.

Department of Education and Science (1978) *Special Educational Needs* (The Warnock Report), London: HMSO.

Department of Education and Science (1989) *Discipline in Schools* (The Elton Report), London: HMSO.

Docking, J. (1990) *Managing Behaviour in the Primary School*, London: David Fulton Publishers.

Galloway, D. and Goodwin, C. (1987) *The Education of Disturbing Children*, London: Longman.

Hanko, G. (1985) *Special Needs in Ordinary Classrooms*, Oxford: Blackwell.

Her Majesty's Inspectorate of Schools (1978) *Truancy* and *Behavioural Problems in Some Urban Schools*, London: Information Division of the Department of Education and Science.

Laslett, R. (1977) *Educating Maladjusted Children*, London: Granada.

Lawson, J. and Silver, H. (1973) *A Social History of Education in England*, London: Methuen & Co.

Lowe, P. (1988) *Responding to Adolescent Needs*, London: Cassell.

Perry, C. (1980) *Boy in the Blitz* (illustrated ed) Farnham Common, Bucks: Colin A. Parry Ltd.

Piaget, J. (1959) *The Language and Thought of the Child*, London: Routledge and Kegan Paul.

Rutter, M. (1979) *Fifteen Thousand Hours*, London: Open Books.

Topping, K. (1983) *Educational Systems for Disruptive Adolescents*, Beckenham: Croom Helm.

Watkins C. and Wagner, P. (1987) *School Discipline – the Whole School Approach*, Oxford: Blackwell.

White, R. (1980) *Absent with Cause*, London: Routledge & Kegan Paul.

White, R. and Brockington, T. (1978) *In and Out of School*, London: Routledge & Kegan Paul.

Widlake, P. (1983) *How to Reach the Hard to Teach*, Milton Keynes: Open University Press.

Index